KENYA & TANZANIA

THE INSIDER'S GUIDE

KENYA & TANZANIA

THE INSIDER'S GUIDE

CONTENTS

AUTHOR'S NOTE

I have always wanted to spend an extended period of time in Kenya and Tanzania. I have visited both countries many times over the years, usually as a guide while on safari, but always visiting specific destinations, and never staying long enough to absorb the extent of the incredible wilderness found beyond the settled regions, the immense biodiversity, or the rich cultural heritage. Writing this book has, at last, made it possible. It has allowed me the opportunity to reach those far-flung corners that one can only explore on an extended road trip. The experience was truly thrilling, and all the more memorable in that it allowed me to meet and spend time with some incredible people, both local and expatriate. It has never been the ambition of the *Insider's* series to provide a complete picture of the countries visited; but I do hope that in this, the third in the series, I have managed to portray something of the vibrancy of Kenya and Tanzania.

Page 1: *Ballooning over the Masai Mara.*
Pages 2–3: *The silhouette of a Maasai man is an enduring image of East Africa.*
Pages 4–5: *Buffalo on the plains of Amboseli National Park.*
Opposite: *As depicted in this street scene in Arusha, aspects of traditional life continue alongside the more modern world in Kenya and Tanzania.*

"I URGE ALL OF YOU TO PAY YOUR TAXES AND SET OUR COUNTRY FREE"

H.E. President Mwai Kibaki.

Welcome to
KENYA & TANZANIA

Of all the regional African groupings that exist in various contexts – such as geographical, political, economic (see below) – the East African one that pairs Kenya and Tanzania somehow seems the most natural. Being **agreeable neighbours** with sound bilateral political relations is a good enough reason, but the confirming factors come from all that they share: Swahili and English as their main languages, a similar history of migration, conquest and colonialism, and the remarkable natural heritage extending across both countries that acts as the bonding agent. It is hardly surprising that visitors to the region will often include Kenya and Tanzania on the same itinerary.

The relative political stability of both countries in an otherwise turbulent region is also important. Despite long-standing and ongoing conflicts in their neighbours Rwanda, Burundi, Democratic Republic of Congo, Sudan, Ethiopia and Somalia, Kenya and Tanzania remain relative **havens of peace**.

But there are nonetheless numerous distinguishing factors. Of these, the most intriguing are the **contrasting political cycles** and socio-economic fortunes each has experienced since independence. Kenya was already established as a regional power when its first president, Jomo Kenyatta, started to set the country up for the future. He attracted widespread approval and investment with his conciliatory political tone and promotion of an open economy. Almost 15 years later, and still under the same party banner, Daniel Arap Moi took over. It was not long after this that the rot set in. His more than 20 years of autocratic rule were characterised by cronyism and maladministration, and by the time he left government in 2002, institutionalised corruption had seriously damaged the political and moral fabric of Kenya. The early promise had been squandered, and growth and development stifled. In some quarters his departure was greeted with euphoria, and the country as a whole had high hopes for widespread political and economic reforms.

Tanzania in many ways has been the mirror image. At independence it was not nearly as developed or as significant a regional player as its northern neighbour. The country began its independence by heading even deeper into the political and economic wilderness. No sooner had he been sworn in as the first post-colonial

president than Julius Nyerere took the country on a long and arduous path of severe socialism. His programme of rural agricultural co-operation was fashioned around the principles of what he labelled 'Ujamaa', or 'familyhood'. It was not successful and eventually became extremely unpopular. Nyerere left office in 1985, and although it was at least another decade before the country had rid itself of his thinking, Tanzania's fortunes have been steadily improving ever since. He was successful, however, in one sense: Tanzania is a more united country than Kenya, and does not suffer the latter's ethnic tensions.

Today, both countries are still regarded as underdeveloped, and they labour under mountains of international debt, but the immediate future holds different prospects for each. Kenya remains the regional centre of NGO and multinational activity, but the government of Mwai Kibaki continues to struggle with the legacy left by Moi. Corruption remains endemic, political infighting is a prominent feature, and economic growth and investment are sluggish. Two **critical indicators**: a recent AIG International report estimated that over 55% of citizens live in abject poverty; and GDP per capita has fallen by an annual average of 0.6% since 1990. These highlight the poor record of the country, and the magnitude of the challenges ahead.

Tanzania is still listed as one of the world's poorest countries and relies heavily on foreign aid, yet there is a far more **positive buzz** about the place. The economy has grown at nearly 5% per annum over the last decade and is now moving along at over 6%. Infrastructure development is taking place across the country and multinationals are setting up shop. In the World Economic Forum's 2003/4 Growth Competitiveness Index, Tanzania was ranked 69th, well above Kenya's 83rd position.

The challenges Kenya faces to regain its position of dominance in the greater East African region are by no means insurmountable. The country is strategically placed geographically, it has a reasonably developed industrial base, a communications and banking infrastructure, and a relatively large middle class that is both well-educated and affluent. With its free press and open democracy, the electorate should be able to bring its wishes to bear. Tanzania's major challenge will be to reduce poverty and spread growth and investment to the far-flung regions of the country, rather than in just a few northerly nodes, as at present.

For visitors, much of this merely serves as interesting background information. Both countries have well developed tourism industries that are second only to their agricultural sectors, so you are going to be **truly welcomed** and looked after in a thoroughly professional way. The signs of poverty and under-development are there for all to see; but the warm-hearted people and the immense beauty and diversity of landscapes and wildlife are likely to be the more enduring memories. Welcome to Kenya and Tanzania.

Previous spread: *A billboard plea from the Kenyan President in downtown Nairobi.*
Below: *Maasai women wear intricate head and neck pieces with the different clans and families often using characteristic styles and colours.*
Right: *Nairobi skyline.*

The original safari

The word **safari** has become synonymous with almost any form of excursion into the African bush, and is quite possibly the most used term within wildlife travel circles. It was derived from Arabic and absorbed into the Swahili language to describe a journey or expedition, before passing into the English vocabulary.

At the height of the **Swahili civilisation** in East Africa, its common usage was probably to describe the caravans that journeyed from the coast into the heart of Africa to collect ivory, gold, slaves and other goods for trade. The European adventurers, explorers and missionaries, many of them English-speakers, who arrived in the 18th and 19th centuries embraced a similar form of travel – heading out on foot with a caravan that included tons of equipment shouldered by masses of porters and, at times, domestic beasts. They too no doubt used the word safari when describing their endeavours, and in this way the word became part of the English language.

The leap into the lexicon of tourism would have come with the advent of large hunting expeditions, which became the favourite pastime of so many colonials during the early 1900s. This was followed by the beginnings of photographic or non-hunting tourism into the wilderness, which has spawned what is today loosely known as the safari industry. Throughout East and southern Africa it's a **substantial industry**, a cornerstone of conservation and of the economies of many of these countries. While the word is now used generically, many operators still offer safaris based on the so-called traditional concepts: providing a mobile or overland trip where the camp and all its equipment is moved from day to day.

Some statistics will indicate how important tourism has become: in Tanzania, annual arrivals between 1990 and 2003 have grown from 153 000 to 575 235 visitors. The government has set the target of luring one million tourists by 2010. In Kenya, arrivals have risen from 61 000 visitors at independence to over one million today.

So, enjoy your safari or, as the locals would say, *safari njema!*

What is East Africa?

The term East Africa is widely used as a **regional reference**, but it does not always necessarily refer to the same group of countries. Since the colonial era, writers, historians, politicians, economists and geographers have variously bracketed a number of countries together under the name of East Africa.

The term was first used by the colonial powers prior to World War I when Kenya was officially known as British East Africa, and Tanzania as German East Africa. Following the war, but before independence, these two countries and Uganda were loosely grouped as East Africa because they shared a common currency (the East African shilling), airline (East African Airways) and co-operated on various governmental and economic issues under the guidance of the British. The grouping was formalised after independence, when the East African Economic Community was established. The arrangement fell apart in the 1970s, but was revived in 2004 with the signing of the East Africa Community (EAC) Treaty between the same three countries.

When the region is described in **geographical terms**, particularly with reference to the Great Rift Valley, then Ethiopia, Eritrea, Djibouti and Somalia are often considered to be part of East Africa. Other sources refer to the Swahili-speaking regions of East Africa, which include Rwanda and Burundi. From a tourism perspective, the safari industry has generally regarded East Africa as consisting of Kenya and Tanzania only; hence these two countries are the ones that form the subject matter for this book.

Opposite: *The cultural experience has become an integral part of any East African safari.*

Below: *Viewing flamingos in Lake Magadi, in the Ngorongoro Crater.*

Proudly tanzanite

Along with Sri Lanka and Brazil, East Africa is regarded as one of the world's richest areas for gem deposits. Because of the ancient and cataclysmic geological processes that have shaped its landscapes, **more than 40 varieties of gemstones** are to be found, with deposits concentrated in the central and northern regions of Tanzania and the southern regions of Kenya. Among the favourites are rubies, sapphires, emeralds and garnet, but of them all, the most sought-after is the rare endemic stone known as **tanzanite**.

This exceptionally beautiful, delicate and almost transparent blue gem was first discovered in 1967 amongst the Merelani Hills near Arusha by Jumanne Mhero Ngoma, a Maasai herdsman. The find created a chaotic rush with random mining occurring until the government instituted a lease system in the early 1990s. Today tanzanite is the pride of the nation, and because it is still reasonably affordable, the stone is one of the most popular souvenirs for foreign visitors.

• Tanzanite is a sapphire-blue variety of the mineral zoisite, which is part of the epidote mineral group that comes from metamorphic rocks dating back over 500 million years.

• It is one of the most recently discovered gemstones, and although insignificant deposits have been found in Kenya and central Tanzania, the only known viable commercial deposit occurs where it was first found, outside Arusha. Geologists have estimated that the reserves will last another three to four decades.

• The stone possesses the unusual quality of being trichroic, which means that it shows different colours when viewed along each of its three crystal axes. The colours it may display range from blues through to purple and even browns.

• Reputedly, the name was first suggested by Henry B. Platt from Tiffany's in New York where it was first displayed, and was accepted by then Tanzanian president Julius Nyerere, who also accorded the gem national status.

• To the locals, tanzanite was formed as an act of God when lightning set the rocks of the surrounding hills alight with huge fires. In the cooling process, the rock buried deep inside turned blue, and it is these rocks that are mined today.

• The most precious varieties are those that display the deepest blues, almost resembling sapphire.

Below: *Mohammed Matata, a gem cutter from Swala Gem Traders in Arusha, works with tanzanite, a gemstone unique to Tanzania.*
Opposite: *A market scene in Morogoro.*

A first for Kenya and Africa

In October 2004, Kenyan ecologist **Wangari Maathai** was awarded the **Nobel Peace Prize**, making her the first African woman to win this prestigious award, and the first person to win it for environmental work. In making the award, the committee praised her 'holistic approach to sustainable development that embraces democracy, human rights and women's rights'. Maathai has been tirelessly championing environmental issues for her whole working life, mostly through the highly successful **Green Belt Movement** she established in 1977. The movement focuses on preventing deforestation, on the planting of trees and soil rehabilitation while promoting sustainable living amongst the nation's people. Maathai has not always held the status of a national hero. Under the past President Daniel Arap Moi, she suffered at the hands of the police and even spent time in jail for her efforts. She now sits in parliament as an MP for her home town.

Footnote: The spellings Maasai and Masai are used throughout the book. The correct usage is as follows – Maasai when referring to the people, and Masai when referring to a place.

Opposite: *A villager transports palm matting to a market on the outskirts of Dar es Salaam.*
Above: *Maasai men gather on market day in the Ngorongoro Conservation Area.*

be ENTICED

East Africa can lay claim to being the **continent's most enticing region**. It is blessed with immense environmental diversity ranging from alpine mountain-tops, a mosaic of forest and woodland types and the continent's most expansive savannahs, to deserts and tropical-island marine habitats. Anchored by the **Great Rift Valley**, which provides for some of the most spectacular scenery, these sublime land- and seascapes play host to a cultural and wildlife heritage second to none. It's an exceptional mix, which at the very least should persuade you to book a return safari.

Previous spread: *Flamingos feeding in the early morning light of Lake Nakuru.*

Below: *A typical Serengeti setting – vast grass plains interspersed with scattered woodland and granite kopjes.*

Tanzania

Being substantially larger and less developed than Kenya, Tanzania is a more adventurous destination, and with most of the region's remaining expansive wilderness areas found here, there are many more 'off the beaten track' options.

WILD KATAVI

This has to be one of Africa's most enthralling national parks, and most certainly one of Tanzania's wildlife highlights. It's **remote, wild and untrammelled**, and the game-viewing is superb. A few days based at Chada Katavi on a game drive or on foot is a wilderness experience you'll never forget.

GREYSTOKE AND THE CHIMPS

Greystoke Mahale offers the region's ultimate **primate experience.** Mornings are spent in search of wild chimpanzees amongst the lowland forests of the Mahale Mountains, and afternoons are for lazing on sandy shores, spotting those elusive endemic forest birds or sailing the lake's vast waters. And the camp, situated on a private beach overlooking Lake Tanganyika, also happens to be one of East Africa's finest. This is a hideaway that's private, romantic and offers solitude, far removed from the troubles of a hectic world.

THE SERENGETI MIGRATION

Whether it's the river crossings, the calving season or the rut, the vast savannah and woodland habitats of the Serengeti play host to the planet's **most awesome wildlife spectacle.** Wildebeest are the star attraction, but zebra and gazelle add to the almost two million animals involved in this ongoing mass search for greener pastures. Depending on the season, you can be based at one of the eco-lodges, or follow the herds with a private mobile safari.

CLIMB AFRICA'S HIGHEST PEAK

Mt Kilimanjaro is the pinnacle of Africa, and the highest free-standing mountain on the planet. It's a **non-mountaineer's dream**, as no experience is required to scale its summit. With its five vegetation zones, plus spectacular glaciers and the most stunning of views, this mountain just has to be climbed.

THE SOUTHERN CIRCUIT

Far removed from the busier northern circuit, and quite different in their habitats and landscapes, the Selous and Ruaha reserves offer an **exciting and more secluded alternative** for the true wildlife enthusiast. Both areas are expansive, and have a selection of fantastic smaller lodges offering game drives, river trips and walks. The Selous is Africa's largest protected area, with great game viewing, including the best chance of seeing wild dog in East Africa.

IN THE LAND OF GIANTS

Tarangire National Park is a must, particularly during the dry season. It is less visited than the more renowned parks to its north, but just as impressive. The landscape mix of hilly savannahs and marshland is dominated by large herds of elephant, **imposing baobab tree forests** and some of the most gigantic termite mounds to be found anywhere.

ZANZIBAR AND PEMBA

Ideally, these mysterious palm-lined tropical islands, once the commercial and cultural centre of Swahili civilisation, should be a stand-alone destination. If your time is limited, at the very least spend a few days **strolling the narrow alleyways of Stone Town**, or soaking in the sun and diving the warm azure waters. It's the perfect way to end a safari.

LITTLE SWITZERLAND

Inexplicably, the Usumbara Mountains are a destination that is seldom mentioned, yet the range makes for a charming and extremely affordable diversion from the wildlife safari circuit, particularly for locals and for those travelling by vehicle. Head for Muller's Mountain Lodge and a world of **forested peaks**, hiking, mountainbiking and rural tranquillity.

Kenya

This is the true birthplace of the 'safari', and no one does the traditional version better than the Kenyan operators. It does receive many more visitors than Tanzania, but the incredible diversity and the unique cultural experiences that accompany almost every destination more than compensate for the throng at some national parks.

TAKE TO THE CHYULU HILLS ON HORSEBACK

Although adjoining Amboseli, one of Kenya's busiest national parks, and only 200 kilometres from Nairobi, the Chyulu Hills still have a blissful remoteness about them. Escape to Ol Donya Wuas, a wonderfully homely private lodge on a group ranch, and spend the day on horseback, or set out on a fly-camping circuit to explore the **volcanic hills and endless grass plains**. Vehicles and hiking are also options, but nothing beats the exhilaration of roaming on horseback.

FREE YOUR SPIRIT AT MANDA BAY

This private island lodge is Kenya's coastal paradise. There's no over-the-top glitz or glamour here, just the epitome of barefoot beach luxury, which makes Manda Bay the perfect place to relax and free your spirit. A magnificent **60-foot traditional dhow** is available for hire, comfortably fitted for sailing sleep-outs, plus all the water sport options; and you will dine on some of the most sumptuous seafood meals served anywhere along the entire coast.

FLAMINGOS AND RHINO AT LAKE NAKURU

Join a Rob Carr-Hartley mobile safari in this gem of a park and become the audience for Kenya's very own wildlife spectacle. At times, **over a million flamingos and tens of thousands of pelicans** play the starring roles, offering fantastic viewing and great photo opportunities; and when bird boredom sets in, the country's best sightings of rhino and leopard will fill the remainder of your day.

BRILLIANT BIRDING

Because of its continental location and incredible diversity of habitats, East Africa offers birders a **species list of a lifetime**. While Tanzania has a nominally higher species count, Kenya provides a more convenient destination for sightings. Highlights include

Pages 22–23: *The Barabaig people are found mostly in the central regions of northern Tanzania.*
Above: *The front deck view at Loisaba Lodge in Laikipia overlooks this waterhole.*
Opposite: *The swimming pool view from Elsa's Kopje in Meru National Park.*

Above: *A sunset dhow cruise from Manda Bay.*
Below: *Dodo's Tower at Hippo Point on the shores of Lake Naivasha.*

the flamingo lakes of the Great Rift Valley, the endemic forest species of Kakamega and Arabuko-Sokoke, the woodland rarities of Meru, Amboseli and other national parks, and the **spectacular cormorant and heron colonies** found on Lake Victoria.

MARVEL AT THE MASAI MARA

The most northerly region of the greater Serengeti/ Mara ecosystem is undoubtedly Kenya's best-known tract of wilderness. It's pure savannah and always **teeming with wildlife**, but the peak period for the migration crossings is July through October. Whether you are based in one of the eco-lodges, or on a mobile safari, it's a wildlife marvel not to be missed.

AT YOUR LEISURE ON LAMU ISLAND

Take a step back in time, and spend a few days in **Swahili style** at Salama or Azania House. Situated between the bustling waterfront and the main alley-way behind, these two adjoining mansions, recently restored with exquisite attention to detail, make for a perfect base from which to explore Lamu Town and the legacy of traditional Swahili life.

THE UNTAMED NORTH

Stretching from Samburu National Park, through the Mathews Range and up to Lake Turkana, this is Kenya's most rugged and remote country, as well as its most enthralling. The wildlife is surprisingly abundant, the cultural diversity is amazing, and the landscapes are hauntingly beautiful. Start in rustic luxury at Bedouin Camp on the edge of Samburu, and then head north with a mobile operator to the **stark shores of the 'Jade Sea'**.

LAIKIPIA

For wildlife enthusiasts, the privately owned and managed ranches and lodges of Laikipia are a safari destination in themselves. Noted for their successful wildlife management principles, and with what are reputed to be Kenya's only growing regional wildlife populations, the lodges of Borana, Loisaba or Lewa Downs will offer a **more secluded safari alternative** to the national parks and reserves.

Khangas and khikois, both traditional garments along the East African coastline, are for sale on most large beaches.

A fruit seller on the beach of Diani in southern Kenya.

The Orma people of northern Kenya live in large, distinctively domed dwellings.

Lake Eyasi in
northern Tanzania is a
great 'off-the-beaten-
track' destination.

from SKELETONS
to SAFARIS

Overview

The Great Rift Valley has long been regarded as a strong candidate for the title of 'Cradle of Humankind'. This is based on a significant number of discoveries made by palaeontologists and archaeologists, most notably the world-renowned Leakey family, over the last 75 years. A number of factors favourable to hominid development have provided supporting evidence: for example, the moderate climate, the diversity of habitats including the vast grass plains and various water sources, and an abundance of food and shelter.

Although humankind's beginnings were millions of years ago, and untold history and development has taken place since then, these same environmental factors are still at play today, and they provide the ideal conditions and features that make Kenya and Tanzania two of the outstanding safari destinations in the world.

Previous spread: *Elephants and spectacular scenery in Samburu and Buffalo Springs national parks.*
Left: *A Maasai school in the Ngorongoro Conservation Area.*
Below: *A mural of Tanzania's founding president – Julius K Nyerere, left – and the incumbent President – Rais Benjamin W Mkapa.*

Kenya and Tanzania, with Ethiopia, are the nations gouged by the Great Rift Valley, which is regarded as one of the most probable sites of humankind's beginnings. Archaeological expeditions have unearthed human fossils dating back almost 2 million years in Tanzania's Olduvai Gorge (*Australopithecus boisei*, also known as the 'nutcracker man'), and hominid footprints at Laetoli, which are thought to be over 3.5 million years old. In Kenya, the shores of Lake Turkana have yielded an unparalleled diversity of hominid species representing almost 4 million years of evolution.

Prehistoric East Africa was inhabited by hunter-gatherers and various Stone Age cultures. The first outsiders to arrive in the region, around 3000 BC, were Cushitic-speaking agro-pastoralists, who moved southwards from present-day Ethiopia and Sudan. They were followed in far larger numbers by the Bantu speakers who came from West and Central Africa, and the Nilotic peoples moving south down the Nile Valley. Most of the immigrants settled in the interior, particularly along the Great Rift Valley and around the great lakes. These influxes introduced livestock herding and metal technology and founded numerous powerful kingdoms, as well as some of the present cultural and language groups. The migrations were to continue well into the 16th and 17th centuries, when groups such as the Maasai arrived.

From about 100 AD to 1000 AD, Arab, Omani and Persian traders began sailing the coastline, in the process establishing trading posts and the first urban settlements on the mainland and the offshore islands. They mixed with the local African groups, and introduced Islam to these coastal people. The **Afro-Islamic Swahili** culture began to take root. The word Swahili is derived from the Arabic word *sawahil*, meaning 'of the coast'. Although dominated by Arabic and Persian influences, the culture has incorporated strong elements from African and Asian cultures too.

Factfile – Tanzania

Area (includes Zanzibar Archipelago)	945 087 square kilometres
Population	34.6 million (2002 census)
Population density	36.6 per square kilometre
Population growth rate	2.0% (World Bank 2003)
Urban population	35.2%
Capital city	Dodoma
Principal cities and towns	Dar es Salaam, Mwanza, Tanga, Mbeya, Arusha, and Zanzibar Town
Coastline	1 424 kilometres
National protected areas	28% of the country
Independence	9 December 1961
Unification with Zanzibar	27 April 1964
Official languages	Kiswahili and English
Currency	Tanzania Shilling
Economic growth rate	6.3% p.a. (2004)
Annual GDP	US$ 10.2 billion (2004)
Gross National Income	US$ 290 per capita (2004)
Poverty	35% live below the national poverty line
Human Development Index	Ranked 162nd out of 177 states

• The **United Republic of Tanzania** consists of the mainland, formerly known as Tanganyika, the offshore islands of Unguja (Zanzibar) and Pemba, collectively known as the Zanzibar Archipelago, and a number of smaller islands and islets.

• The United Republic was established on 26 April 1964 when Tanganyika and Zanzibar, hitherto separate independent countries, merged. The country has a single national constitution, but in 1979 the Revolutionary Council of Zanzibar adopted a separate constitution governing Zanzibar's internal administration.

• Tanzania is **a multi-party democracy** with presidential and constitutional elections held every five years. Legislative power is exercised through the Parliament, which sits in the National Assembly. The Assembly has 268 seats, of which 231 are elected, 10 are nominated by the President and 27 are reserved for women. The President is Head of State and Head of the Government. Zanzibar has its own House of Representatives (81 members), which deals with internal matters only.

The **country's economy** is beginning to diversify, but agriculture has always been its backbone.

This sector is the principal employer with over 80% of the population reliant on it in some form, and it accounts for almost 45% of GDP (2003). The sector is also a major export earner, with the principal crops being coffee, cashew nuts, sisal, tea, cotton, tobacco and cloves. The horticulture sector, particularly the export of cut flowers, is a major growth sector. Subsistence crops include cassava, beans, maize, rice and bananas.

• **The industry and manufacturing sector** is the second-largest employer and contributes close to 16% of GDP (2003). The major activities are processed foodstuffs, beer and beverages, cement production, textiles and light engineering.

• **The services sector,** of which tourism is the major component, contributes approximately 38% of GDP (2003), and is one of the fastest-growing sectors of the economy.

• **Tanzania is blessed with substantial mineral deposits.** Gemstones, gold, silver, tin, coal, diamonds, iron ore, nickel and natural glass are the most important natural resources. This sector is still relatively undeveloped, but has vast potential for the country. Mining, particularly for gold and platinum, is targeted as a major growth industry. The government also wants to promote value-added industries in this sector, particularly for gemstones.

• **Principal trading partners** (2003) for exports are the United Kingdom, France, Japan, India, Netherlands and Kenya; and for imports, South Africa, Japan, the United Kingdom, the United Arab Emirates, the United States, Kenya, India and China.

• **The independent judiciary** is based on English common law combined with elements of tribal and Islamic law. The law is administered through a system of Primary and District Courts subordinate to the High Court and Court of Appeals in Dar es Salaam. Zanzibar has a number of tribunals covering land, housing and commerce, as well as Islamic Courts, which adjudicate on Muslim family issues.

• Tanzania is a **secular state** with at least 50% of mainland Tanzanians being followers of Christianity, chiefly Anglican and Roman Catholic, and approximately 30% Islamic. In Zanzibar, 96% are followers of the Islamic faith. Traditional belief systems are still strong in the rural areas.

• **Education** at primary level is free and though it is officially compulsory, it is not enforced. The UN Human Development Report puts the adult literacy rate at 75.1%. The country has three major universities and a number of technical and business colleges.

• Tanzania is a **non-aligned state** and a member of the United Nations, the Southern African Development Community, the African Union, the East African Community Treaty, the Commonwealth and the World Trade Organization.

• **The national flag** consists of four colours. Green in the upper left triangle represents the land and its resources, while the blue at the bottom right represents the lakes, rivers and sea. A black stripe with gold borders crosses the flag diagonally representing the people and the country's mineral wealth.

• **Tanzania's national symbol** is the independence torch, and the motto, *Uhuru na Umoja*, means 'Freedom and Unity'.

A BRIEF HISTORY OF TANZANIA

10 000 BC: The early ancestors of today's Hadzabe and Sandawe people are known to have been Tanzania's first inhabitants. Much like the Bushmen of Southern Africa, they are true hunter-gatherers and speak a click language. Remnant populations still survive today, although their traditional lifestyles have been much altered.

1498–1520: In 1498, the Portuguese arrived as the first Europeans on these shores, and by 1506 they had established control of Tanzania's coastline as well as the islands of Zanzibar, Pemba and Mafia. Though they did not always enjoy good fortune, the Portuguese remained as an influential force for 200 years.

1698: Defeated by the Omani Arabs, the Portuguese were driven out of Zanzibar and lost control of the mainland coast. The Al-Busaid dynasty set about establishing control of the East African coastline using Zanzibar as a base. This also heralded the beginning of a period of almost 200 years that was the height of the ivory and slave trade, with Stone Town at its centre.

±1840–late 1800s: This was the period of exploration and the beginnings of European colonial rule.

In Tanzania, approximately 30% of the population is of the Islamic faith, while in Kenya it is approximately 6%.

The twin spires of St Joseph's Cathedral are a prominent feature of the Stone Town skyline.

Mt Kilimanjaro was first described to the outside world, Richard Burton and John Speke braved the interior to reach Lake Tanganyika, David Livingstone campaigned for an end to the slave trade and numerous missions were established across the country.

1861–1862: Zanzibar moved to declare its independence from Oman and became separated from the Arabic state in 1862 with the help of the British, who had begun expanding their interests in the region in the prior decades. Omani Sultans continued to rule, but under British protection.

1884: Karl Peters began the period of German colonialism by signing various treaties with local chiefs, initially acting without a mandate. Peters then got the backing of the German government for the establishment of his German East Africa Company which offered German government protection as part of the deal for land and trading rights.

1890–1891: The British and Germans signed a treaty formalising their respective territories. The British took control of Zanzibar as a full Protectorate and the German government assumed full control of what was then mainland German East Africa, establishing its headquarters in Dar es Salaam.

1905–1907: Colonial rule was harsh, and this led to the Maji Maji rebellion against the Germans, fought primarily in the south. *Maji* means 'water' in Swahili, and the rebels believed that German bullets would dissolve into water when fired. Over 100 000 people died in the rebellion against forced labour and miserable living conditions on the plantations. Many regard the Maji Maji period as the beginnings of Tanzanian nationalism.

1914–1918: During the early months of the First World War the Germans sank a British battleship in the Battle of Tanga. After Germany lost the war, German East Africa was handed over to the British under a League of Nations mandate. The region became known as Tanganyika and over the following decades, the occupiers introduced colonial administrative systems.

1948–1954: In 1948, the Tanganyika Africa Association (TAA) was formed to represent growing political opposition to colonial rule, and in 1953 the body elected Julius Nyerere, a teacher and one of only two Tanganyikans with an international university degree, as its president. In 1954, the TAA adopted its own constitution, with independence firmly on the agenda. It also changed its name to the Tanganyika African National Union.

1961–1964: In May 1961, Tanganyika became autonomous, and full independence was achieved in December of that year. In December 1962 it became a Republic, with Julius Nyerere as the first President. Zanzibar gained independence from Omani rule in December 1963. In April 1964, the Omani Sultanate was overthrown in a bloody revolution, and Zanzibar and Tanganyika merged to form the United Republic of Tanzania.

1967: Nyerere drew up the Arusha Declaration, containing his vision for the people of Tanzania: a strong dose of socialism based on self-reliance. Known as Ujamaa (Swahili for 'familyhood'), the programme sought to promote education, economic co-operation and social equality by bringing Tanzanian families together under a traditional village system. In the process, over 80% of Tanzania's rural population was moved into thousands of planned villages. In the end it proved to be widely unpopular, not least because it was an economic failure.

1978–1979: Ugandan forces under control of the dictator Idi Amin invaded north-eastern Tanzania. Tanzanian troops reclaimed the territory in 1979 and invaded Uganda, which culminated in the toppling of Amin's government.

1980–1985: In 1980, Nyerere was elected to a fifth term, but with declining economic fortunes and growing discontent over his leadership, he stepped down from the Presidency in 1985 and was replaced by Ali Hassan Mwinyi. Nyerere died in 1999.

1992–1995: After changes to the constitution introduced multi-party politics in 1992, Benjamin Mkapa was elected to the Presidency in the first elections, held in 1995.

1998: The American embassies in Nairobi and Dar es Salaam were destroyed by unknown bombers, with severe consequences to the economies of the region, particularly the tourism industry.

2000: Mkapa was re-elected.

Factfile – Kenya

Area	586 600 square kilometres
Population	31.5 million (2002 census)
Population density	53.6 per square kilometre
Population growth rate	1.2%
Urban population	39%
Capital city	Nairobi
Principal cities and towns	Mombasa, Kisumu, Nakuru and Eldoret
Coastline	550 kilometres
National protected areas	11% as national and other protected areas
Independence	12 December 1963
Official language	English
National language	Kiswahili
Currency	Kenya Shilling
Economic growth rate	2.4% (2004)
Annual GDP	US$ 12.5 billion (2003)
Gross National Income	US$ 390 per capita (2003)
Poverty	58% live below the national line
Human Development Index	148th out of 177 states

• The **Republic of Kenya** is a multi-party democracy with a single chamber known as the National Assembly. There are 224 seats, 210 elected every five years by popular vote, 12 nominated by parliament and 2 ex-officio members. The President is both the chief of state and head of government.

• Kenya has an extremely **uneven population distribution.** The dry north and north-east have densities as low as 2 persons per square kilometre, while in the fertile west this rises to over 120 per square kilometre.

• **Agriculture** is the backbone of Kenya's economy, and almost 75% of Kenyans rely on the sector for some form of income. It is the largest foreign exchange earner, accounting for over 50% of income, and it contributes almost 16% of GDP. Tea (Kenya is the world's second largest tea exporter), coffee and cut flowers are the major exports. Other export crops include sisal, tropical fruits, pyrethrum, and vegetables.

• **Industry and manufacturing** account for almost 20% of GDP. The major sectors include soda-ash, cement, food processing, light industry and oil refining.

• Led by the tourism industry, **the services sector** contributes the largest component of GDP, totalling almost 65%. Tourism is also the second largest foreign exchange earner.

• Kenya's **largest trading partners** for exports are Uganda, the United Kingdom, the United States, Netherlands and Pakistan; for imports, they are the United Arab Emirates, Saudi Arabia, South Africa and the United Kingdom.

• Kenya **is a secular state** with a large Christian following. Almost 38% of the population is Protestant and 30% Catholic. Islam, found predominantly along the coastline, accounts for 6%, and traditional beliefs are commonly practised in most rural areas.

• **The judicial system** is based on Kenyan statutory law, which has been compiled from Kenyan and English common law, tribal law and Islamic law. The system operates through various local and district Magistrate's Courts, the High Court and the Court of Appeals. Islamic Courts are appointed to deal with local customary issues between Muslims. Customary courts were abolished in 1967.

• Kenya has a relatively large middle class and a literacy rate of over 85%. **The education system** offers 14 years of schooling, with 8 years free at primary level. There are two major universities and a number of polytechnics and colleges.

• Kenya is a **non-aligned state** and a member of the Commonwealth, United Nations, African Union, East African Community Treaty and the World Trade Organization.

• **The national flag** is covered in equal proportions by three broad horizontal bands of colour: the black on the top represents the people, the red in the middle, the blood shed in the fight for independence, and the green on the bottom, the land and its fertility. The bands are separated by narrow white stripes representing peace and the future. The shield in the centre of the flag represents the pride and traditions of the nation.

• The Lilac-breasted Roller is **Kenya's national bird.**

A BRIEF HISTORY OF KENYA

1498–1528: In 1498, the Portuguese arrived as the first Europeans on these shores. They stopped off at Malindi and within a few years began attacking

Top: *Accompanied by deep rhythmic humming, a Maasai warrior performs the traditional adumu dance.*
Above: *Fort Jesus in Mombasa was built by the Portuguese in 1593.*
Right: *Downtown Nairobi.*

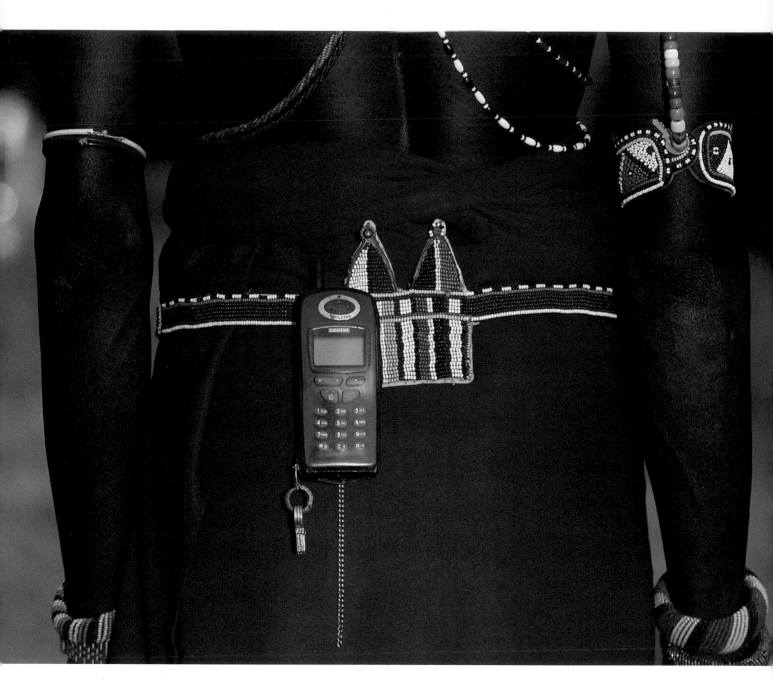

A Samburu warrior from northern Kenya.

a number of Swahili trading cities along the coast. In 1528 they attacked Mombasa and established political and economic dominance in the region. The Portuguese were to remain an influential force along the entire East African coastline for over 200 years.

1593: The Portuguese built Fort Jesus in Mombasa.

Early 1700s–Late 1800s: Ongoing battles with the Omanis began taking their toll, and by 1720, the last of the Portuguese were forced to leave the region. Under the leadership of the Sultan of Oman, based on Zanzibar Island, the Omanis took control of the Kenyan coastline. The ivory and slave trade flourished during this period, reaching its peak in the early to mid 1800s.

1895: As a consequence of the Berlin Conference, Uganda in 1893 and Kenya in 1895 became British Protectorates. The British began building the region's first railway line, linking the interior of these territories to the coast. Over the next few decades, Kenya experienced an influx of white settlers, forcing many African people off their traditional land and into large plantations producing export crops.

1904: Compelled by British authorities, Maasai leaders signed a treaty relinquishing fertile traditional lands to European settler farmers.

1921–1929: Grievances over land ownership, forced removals and economic issues led to the first African political protest movements under the leadership of Harry Thuku. Thuku was later arrested and exiled to Somalia. Under the leadership of Jomo Kenyatta the Kikuyu Central Association was formed, and in 1929 he sailed to England to petition that country's parliament and people for the rights and freedom of his homeland. Kenyatta spent the next 15 years travelling and studying in Europe.

1945: At the end of the Second World War, the British authorities handed out subsidised land to European war veterans. The result was an influx of approximately 60 000 white settlers.

1947–1951: With the Kikuyu people at the forefront, the Mau Mau uprisings began. Guerrillas took an oath that committed them to reclaiming their land and expelling all white settlers from Kenya. The conflict was bloody. Attacks on white farms and police stations resulted in nearly 14 000 deaths, mostly in the central regions of the country.

1953–1959: In 1953, Jomo Kenyatta was charged with directing Mau Mau activities and sentenced to 7 years' hard labour. By 1956 the authorities had crushed the rebellion, detaining all the senior leaders and executing some of them. In 1959, the British administration began returning freehold land titles to Africans.

1960: British authorities agreed to meet with nationalist African leaders, who were subsequently allowed to form political parties. The Kenya African National Union (KANU) was born, with the newly-released Kenyatta as leader.

1963–1964: On 12 December 1963 Kenya became a fully-independent state with Jomo Kenyatta as the country's first President. A year later, he declared the country a one-party state.

1968: Tom Mboya, a Luo leader and opponent of Kenyatta, was assassinated. Riots broke out between the Kikuyu and Luo people.

1978: Jomo Kenyatta died and Daniel Arap Moi succeeded him as Kenya's second President. Moi survived a coup attempt in 1982, and went on to lead the country for 24 years. His autocratic rule was characterised by maladministration, repeated allegations of corruption and suppression of his opponents.

1990: Dr Robert Ouko, a former Foreign Affairs minister who had become a critic of the Moi regime, was murdered.

1992: After amendments to the constitution, Kenya became a multi-party democracy for the first time in its history. Moi won a landslide election victory amid political violence and allegations of vote-rigging.

1998: The American embassies in Nairobi and Dar es Salaam were destroyed by unknown bombers, with severe consequences to the economies of the region, particularly the tourism industry.

2002: Moi resigned and Uhuru Kenyatta, son of the first President, took control of the ruling KANU party. In the parliamentary elections of that year and for the first time since independence, KANU lost. A coalition under the banner of the National Rainbow Coalition (NARC) won a landslide victory and Mwai Kibaki became President. The next elections are due in 2007.

Previous spread:
*Pineapples are grown
commercially along the
coastline of Tanzania.*
This spread:
*Kenya is presently
the second largest
tea-producing nation in
the world. This picker
works on an estate in the
Kericho district of south-
western Kenya.*

47

the GREAT RIFT VALLEY

There is no region of Africa that has been more contorted, ruptured and seared by the geological might of nature than the east of the continent. The scars of those **tumultuous subterranean processes** are seen today in the immensely diverse topography of the region that is defined by the Great Rift Valley (GRV) and its associated escarpments, volcanoes and lakes.

Changing climatic patterns have also played a shaping role. Over 50 million years ago, tropical forests covered most of the region, but over time, lower rainfall levels and the advent of drier climates, along with massive fires associated with volcanic activity, allowed woodland and vast grass-covered plains to flourish. These expanses, known as savannahs, are as much a characteristic of the GRV as the mountain chains and water systems. Ranging in type from mixed woodland to sweeping carpets of flat-leaved grasses, the savannahs provide nourishment to the **greatest biomass of wildlife** on the continent, which is the prime attraction for the majority of safari visitors.

Although the region's **topography** varies dramatically, it can be summarised as follows:
- **A low-lying coastline** with plains that spread inland, particularly in central and northern Kenya and southern Tanzania.
- **The central highland** regions and mountain ranges of the GRV with two branches, the Western Rift and the Eastern Rift, running on a north/south axis. These ranges include a large number of volcanoes, some of which are still active.
- **Medium altitude plateaus** (between 1 000 and 2 000 metres on average) lying between the 2 branches of the GRV and to the west of the Western Rift.
- **Many lakes,** both saline and freshwater, including the second largest and the second deepest in the world.

Previous spread: *One of the most impressive views of the Great Rift Valley – along the main road from Nairobi to Naivasha.*
Below: *The Kerio Valley in the Great Rift Valley of western Kenya.*

Dynamics of the Great Rift Valley (GRV)

It all began **over two hundred million years ago** when the world consisted of one super-continent known as Pangaea, and natural forces started to split this single landmass. In the process known as **continental drift**, two continents were formed, Laurasia in the north and Gondwana in the south, and then from about 150 million years ago, Gondwana itself began to split, giving rise to South America, India, Australia, Antarctica and Africa, which is the world's second largest continent.

Continental drift is an ongoing process driven by cataclysmic **tectonic activity** that takes place along plate boundaries, the margins that define the present positioning of the world's major land-masses. Secondary boundaries form as fault lines and junctions through upwarping, downwarping and rifting. Some of these may, millions of years into the future, become major new boundaries of their own, which then could give rise to further land-masses.

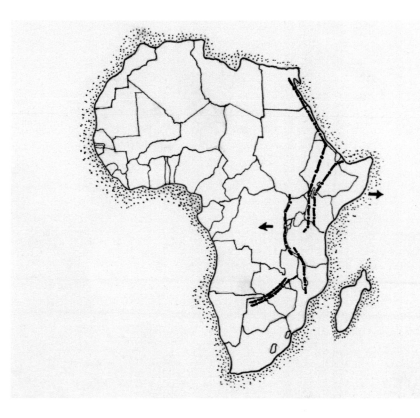

The processes of continental drift have been in action for hundreds of millions of years, but the **formation of the GRV** is a more recent development. Its beginnings go back approximately 25 million years when the Arabian Plate and the African Plate started to shift. In time, the Arabian Peninsula split from Africa, allowing the Red Sea to form. The ongoing tectonic activity has weakened sections of the Earth's crust and given rise to the **East African Rift Zone**, which stretches from the Gulf of Aden down through Ethiopia and into Tanzania and Kenya. The Rift Zone is a more recent spreading area and it also forms the divide for the emerging minor plates, the Nubian Plate to the west and the Somali Plate to the East, that make up the African Plate. As these minor plates have drifted outwards and away from two parallel fault lines, the ground between

has sunk, forming a trough with steep-sided walls. This is the GRV. The Earth's crust has become warped and stretched, and at the weakest points, molten magma from the inner core has forced its way through, giving rise to the numerous volcanoes found in East Africa. This process began in the north shortly after the plates began shifting, and worked its way south. While most of the volcanism occurred before the formation of the GRV, some features, such as Mt Kilimanjaro, have appeared since its formation.

Plate movements and associated geothermal activities continue to shape the GRV. In time, geologists believe that continued subsidence could lead to the land east of the rift zone becoming separated from the continent when ocean water fills the lower lying land, forming a new ocean and land mass.

Factfile

- Regarded as the **largest and longest geographical feature** on Earth, the GRV is reputed to have been the only landmark picked out by the first astronauts entering space.

- It was first described back in the 1890s and then named by the Scottish explorer and geologist, **John Walter Gregory**. In some texts, it is known as the East African Rift Valley, the East African Rift System or the Afro-Arab Rift System.

- It covers **over 6 000 kilometres**, stretching from Jordan in the Middle East into southern Africa as far as the mouth of the Zambezi River in Mozambique.

- The **width of the valley floor** varies from 30 kilometres at its narrowest to almost 100 kilometres, and the depth ranges from below sea level in certain depressions to cliff faces reaching over 1 800 metres.

- Sections of the GRV are often referred to by names specific to their regions. The most ancient of these is the **Abyssinian Rift**, which is the section that starts at the Red Sea and extends down through Ethiopia.

- In East Africa, the GRV consists of two branches that eventually merge in the south of the region. The wider and longer **Eastern Rift** starts where the Red Sea and the Gulf of Aden merge, and passes through the central regions of both Kenya and Tanzania. The narrower and shorter **Western Rift** emerges in southern Sudan and extends along the western borders of Uganda, Rwanda, Burundi and Tanzania before joining the Eastern Rift in the Southern Highlands of Tanzania and northern Malawi.

- South of East Africa, the rift is often known as the **Nyasa Rift**, as it passes through Lake Nyasa in Malawi before entering Mozambique.

- The section of the Eastern Rift that passes through northern Tanzania and into central Kenya is often referred to as the Gregory Rift, after John Walter Gregory. The Western Rift is sometimes referred to as the **Albertine Rift**, as Lake Albert is its most northerly distinctive feature.

- Of the **numerous volcanoes** found along both branches of the GRV, over thirty are still regarded as active or dormant. While there are no records of cataclysmic eruptions, the most recent outpourings have been those of Nyamuragira (2002) and Nyiragongo (2002) in the Virunga Mountains on the edge of the Western Rift. Ol Donyo Lengai (1983) in the Eastern Rift also remains active. The numerous boiling spring sites in East Africa are associated with the volcanic activity.

- The **best-known volcanoes** are Mt Kilimanjaro, Africa's highest point (5 896 metres), Mt Kenya, Africa's second highest point (5 199 metres), Mt Meru, the fifth highest point (4 566 metres), and Mt Elgon in Kenya (4 321 metres). The Ngorongoro Crater (2 200 metres), which is best known for the unique game-viewing experiences within its walls, is part of a greater ecosystem known as the Crater Highlands, which includes the volcanic peaks of Loolmalasin 3 648 metres), Empakaai (3 262 metres), Oldeani (3 216 metres), Lemagurut (3 107 metres), Olmoti (3 100 metres) and Ol Donyo Lengai (2 878 metres).

- The GRV has **over 30 large lakes** and untold smaller crater lakes associated with it. While some are fresh, the majority of these are alkaline, with high concentrations of sodium carbonate. Of Tanzania's total surface area, 54 390 square kilometres are covered by lakes and swamps; in Kenya, 10 700 square kilometres comprise inland water bodies, and a further 3 000 square kilometres wetlands.

- Tanzania's major river is the **Rufiji**, which flows into the Indian Ocean approximately 100 kilometres south of Dar es Salaam. Other major rivers are the Ruvuma in the south, the Pangani in the north, and the Ruaha and Rungwa in the central regions.

- Kenya's major river is the **Tana**, which flows into the Indian Ocean just south of Lamu. Other major rivers include the Athi/Galana system in the south, and the Ewaso Ng'iro in the north.

- The **drainage pattern** for the region has the major river systems draining from the central highlands, either westwards into Lakes Victoria and Tanganyika or eastwards into the Indian Ocean. There are also a number of internal drainage basins, notably those of Lake Eyasi and Lake Rukwa in Tanzania.

- The GRV is home to the **greatest density of wildlife** found on earth.

Late evening light catches Kibo, the central peak on Mt Kilimanjaro, a dormant volcano within the Great Rift Valley.

East Africa's great lakes

For many, the most spectacular features of the GRV are the **region's three great lakes**: Lake Tanganyika in the Western Rift, Lake Nyasa in the Eastern Rift, and Lake Victoria, which lies between the two branches.

Their massive size is a distinguishing feature, as is the vital role they play in providing for the millions of people who live along their shores, but of even greater interest is the unique and **fascinating pisci-fauna** that swims within their waters. There are more fish species in these lakes than in any other lake system in the world, and more fish species in Lake Nyasa alone than in all the North American lakes put together. The fish that dominate are the **cichlids**, a perch-like tropical fish that forms the largest family of fish found on Earth. Ever since David Livingstone collected the first species from Lake Nyasa back in 1861, evolutionary biologists have shown enormous interest, both in the lakes and in their biodiversity. Because each lake spent the greater part of its formation period isolated from most other water bodies, the evolutionary process has resulted in an incredibly **high level of endemism** amongst the fish species found in each individual lake. Characteristically colourful and small in size, the fish species have radiated to occupy almost every niche from the surface to the lowest possible depths, and each group has evolved its own peculiar feeding and breeding habits.

LAKE TANGANYIKA – Formed over 6 million years ago, this lake is regarded as the oldest of the three, and after Lake Baikal in Russia, is the **second-deepest lake in the world** with a maximum depth of 1 470 metres. Lying at the join of the two branches of the GRV, its 34 000 square-kilometre surface area is characterised by its immensely long and narrow shape, which stretches almost 700 kilometres from Burundi in the north to Zambia in the south. At its widest in the central regions, there is a mere 80-kilometre stretch of water between the Democratic Republic of Congo and Tanzania. The Lukuga River, a tributary of the Zaire River, is its only outlet.

Almost 200 fish species have been identified, and since the lake has spent at least half its life isolated from other water systems, 90% of them are endemic, including all 126 cichlid species. The waters are generally warm, but because of the extreme depths, all life occurs in the top 200 metres of water. Below this, the oxygen levels drop dramatically.

LAKE VICTORIA – Strictly speaking, Lake Victoria is not part of the GRV, but because it lies so prominently between the two branches of the rift zone, its presence cannot be ignored. At almost 69 000 square kilometres, this is the **world's second-largest freshwater lake** after Lake Superior in North America. It is also the youngest and shallowest of the three lakes, reaching only 80 metres at its deepest point, and is regarded as the source of the White Nile. Although it is the largest lake in Africa, it has shores in only three countries, Uganda, Tanzania and Kenya.

Despite its prominence, Lake Victoria is under serious threat from human pressures. With naturally nutrient-rich waters, over 500 species of cichlids have been identified, but many of these are now being lost to excessive pollution that has resulted in dangerous levels of nitrogen and phosphorus buildup in the water. Predation by Nile Perch, an exotic species foolishly introduced into the lake in the late 1950s as an additional food source for humans living along the lake's shores, has also become a major problem for the indigenous fish. And to add to the lake's woes, its surface waters suffer from the invasive growth patterns of the water hyacinth, an introduced exotic plant.

LAKE NYASA – Also known as Lake Malawi, the **most southerly of the great lakes** lies within a trough between Malawi on its western shoreline and Tanzania and Mozambique on the east. Its 29 604-square-kilometre surface area makes it the ninth largest lake in the world, with its greatest depth reaching 706 metres along the rocky north-western shore. Of the three lakes, Nyasa has the greatest fish diversity with over 1 000 species identified, including over 450 cichlids, most of them endemic. Much like Victoria, this lake also faces environmental threats as the number of people living along its shores continues to grow. While there are

Fishermen on Lake Nyasa, which along with Lake Victoria and Lake Tanganyika, comprise the three 'great lakes' of East Africa.

14 rivers feeding the lake, the Shire River in the south is the only drainage outlet.

The GRV is also associated with a number of lakes known as **'soda lakes'** because of their high alkaline levels. In Kenya, the best known are lakes Nakuru, Turkana and Magadi, all with high alkalinity, and the **two freshwater ones**, Lake Baringo and Lake Naivasha. In Tanzania there are three well-known alkaline lakes: Manyara, Eyasi and Natron. The alkaline lakes owe their high sodium carbonate levels to earlier volcanic activity and the steep-sided nature of the valley walls that surround them. The volcanic dust settled in these lakes, and, with few drainage outlets, the water became trapped. High evaporation rates over millions of years have left behind tons of mineral salts on the lake floor. While all the lakes attract large numbers of bird species, the alkaline ones are particularly well known for the **impressive flamingo colonies** that collect to feed on the blue-green algae that thrive in the warm-water conditions.

A place of two seasons

For the most part, this is a region of two seasons – **wet and dry** – rather than the four that occur in the temperate zones of the world. This is because large parts of both countries lie within the inter-tropical convergence zone, and the weather patterns here are determined by the associated **two-season monsoons**. Of equal significance is the influence of the diverse topography in creating greatly varying weather conditions at a local level. Throughout the central regions, altitude is the main determinant of rainfall, with Kenya showing greater extremes for both temperature and rainfall ranges. At least 75% of Kenya may be classified as arid or semi-arid, while there is only a small region within the north of Tanzania that experiences semi-arid conditions.

In general, the coastal regions have a **tropical climate**, with hot and humid conditions prevailing, tempered at times by cooling sea breezes. The average temperatures on the coast remain fairly constant throughout the year, ranging from 22 °C to 31 °C. The higher inland plateau regions have a more temperate climate, with far cooler conditions. The average winter temperatures fall between 10 °C and 20 °C, and summer temperatures between 22 °C and 28 °C. Kenya's drier northern and eastern regions can become extremely hot, with daytime temperatures reaching over 40 °C during summer. Generally, the **coolest months** in East Africa are June through to September, while the warmest months are November through to March.

Most of the East African region has **two monsoon-driven rain periods**, the 'short rains' (*mvuli*) that fall during November and into early December, and the 'long rains' (*masika*) that fall from mid-March through to early June. The regions that fall outside of this pattern are the south of Tanzania, which tends to have a single rain season stretching from November to May, and Kenya's northern and eastern arid regions where rainfall is low and erratic. The western land edges along the lakes may receive rainfall throughout the year, with peaks during the period March to September. Tanzania's average annual rainfall varies between 500 millimetres and 1 200 millimetres, while in Kenya the Lake Victoria region averages 1 700 millimetres, the central coastal regions average 1 050 millimetres and the average for the drier northern inland regions is below 300 millimetres. There are highland regions in both countries that at times experience rainfall of over 2 000 millimetres per year.

Below: *The 'great lakes' are the hunting ground for fish, a primary food source for millions of people living along their shores.*
Opposite: *Storm clouds gather over Lake Nyasa.*

en ROUTE

It needs to be said from the outset: East Africa is not as well-suited for road travel as southern Africa. And if you are going to take to the roads, you will most definitely need to have your wits about you when driving in all cities and towns, and on major routes. Kenya undoubtedly has the most brazen and discourteous, and sometimes dangerous, drivers to be found anywhere in southern and East Africa. Perhaps this is due to the frustrations of having to drive on a major road network that can be charitably described as exceedingly poor. In Tanzania, bus drivers tend to travel at alarming speeds, making each bus a potential 'weapon of mass destruction', and there surely cannot be another country on the continent that has more speed-bumps. Every village and town has them, often in unlikely places, and they are seldom sign-posted or marked. They are certainly effective, but they can do serious damage to your vehicle if hit at speed. Because of these hazards, it's best not to travel after dark in either country. Fuel is readily available in all larger towns in both Kenya and Tanzania.

Road perils aside, there will be enough stunning scenery, fascinating village interludes and exciting exploration to make for a memorable trip. Campsites and roadside lodgings are scarce in both countries, except along the coast. Decent food stops are also rare, so your itinerary needs to be reasonably well planned.

Previous spread: *A vegetable stall on the main Mbeya–Dar es Salaam road in Tanzania.*
Top: *En route to Meru in Kenya.*
Bottom: *Honey is commonly sold along the roadside in Tanzania and Kenya.*
Opposite: *A container ship leaves the port of Dar es Salaam, the busiest along the East African coast.*

City to city

East Africa's two major cities, Dar es Salaam (Dar) in Tanzania and Nairobi in Kenya, are linked by the region's busiest road route. It can be done in a full day's drive, but breaking the journey with a night in Arusha is a more comfortable option. An alternative would be to divert for a few nights through the Usumbara Mountains (see page 161), about halfway between Dar es Salaam and Arusha.

When heading for Dar from the south, the main route goes northwards from Mbeya, and passes through the impressive Uluguru and Udzungwa Ranges and the cities of Iringa and Morogoro. There are a number of worthwhile detours and stopovers along the way. In the Southern Highlands, the 100 kilometre or so loop that winds through the Mufindi tea estates and up to the **Highland Lodge** is a must for keen fishermen, horse-riders and birders. A few days here in the crisp rarefied air, with a combination of forested mountain peaks and well-stocked trout dams, makes for a welcome break in the road trip.

Only a few hours' drive south of Dar and lying in the shadows of the Uluguru Mountains is **Mikumi National Park**. This is a small park, but with reasonable game numbers, so a night or two in either Foxes Safari Camp or Vuma Hills, either of which can be reached via a short detour from the main road, is always worth considering.

DAR ES SALAAM

Although Dodoma is the administrative capital, Dar es Salaam, as the **commercial centre and principal port,** is the major city of Tanzania. Known to the locals simply as Dar, its position of prominence today belies an unremarkable early history. While the Omanis and Portuguese were establishing trading cities and spheres of influence all along the coast, Dar es Salaam remained a small fishing village. Its first spurt of development came in 1862 when Sultan Seyyid Majid of Zanzibar began developing the creek as an alternative trading port to Bagamoyo and as a new capital for his empire. Noting that it was somewhat sheltered from the open seas, he named the city Dari-Salama, which loosely translated from Swahili is **'safe refuge' or 'place of peace'.** He died soon after this, and when his brother, Sultan Seyyid Barghash, took over, the fledgling settlement was abandoned.

It was not until 1891, when the colonial German government moved their administrative centre from Bagamoyo to Dar, that the city's economic fortunes began to improve. Having lost the First World War, the Germans were forced to give up control of all their African territories, and the British took over present-day Tanzania. They continued to develop the city along the racial lines established by the Germans; the Europeans along the shorefront that is today Oyster Bay and

Above left: *Early morning traffic along the Msasani Peninsula, Dar es Salaam.*
Above right: *Fishing boats arriving at the main Fish Market in Kivukoni, Dar es Salaam.*

beyond, the Asians and Arabs in the city centre, and the Africans across the creek, in what are today the sprawling townships of Kariakoo and Upanga on the southern fringes of the city.

At independence, Dar was a moderately sized city, but its fortunes slowed as the failures of Nyerere's Ujamaa policy (see From Skeletons to Safaris, page 39) became more apparent. Moving the seat of government to Dodoma in 1973 did not help either, although Dar always remained the commercial centre.

The fortunes of the somewhat steamy, always bustling former capital city, much like those of the country as a whole, are now on the up again. Upgrades and new construction projects are taking place across the city, and the port has become one of the busiest on the East African coastline. This **regeneration** has not gone unnoticed, as many multi-nationals have recently established regional offices in the city. The influx of money has pushed private property, particularly along the seafront, to premium prices, and has begun to attract the designer stores and restaurants that so often indicate boom times.

While the city is not sufficiently appealing to justify a detour, an overnight stop because of flight arrangements may just prove to be a welcome interlude on the safari circuit. Just remember the golden rule – Dar by day is all about the city centre, and Dar by night happens along 'the Peninsula'.

THINGS TO DO

National Museum – Situated next to the Botanical Gardens in the city centre. Displays include those of the 'nutcracker man' and a history of the region's slave trade. Well worth a visit.

Tinga Tinga Artists' Co-operative – This bustling art market with stalls and artists at work is a great place to hang out. It's alongside the Morogoro Store off Haile Selassie road in Oyster Bay.

Casinos – The gambling set will head off to the Sea Cliff Hotel or the Las Vegas Casino on the beachfront in Oyster Bay.

Fish Market – Markets are always a window into the socio-economic conditions of a nation, and this one in Kivukoni near the city centre is a particularly vibrant one. Get there early as the boats arrive from a night of fishing.

WHERE TO STAY

The Royal Palm – Situated in Ohio Street right near the city centre, this large top-class hotel offers all the modern conveniences. Tel: + 255 22 2112416, e-mail: enquiries@adventures.co.za

Holiday Inn – In Garden Street, which is also close to the city centre, but in a quieter neighbourhood. Tel: +255 22 2137575, e-mail: hidar@hidar.co.tz

Protea Hotel Oyster Bay (formerly known as Protea Apartments) – Situated on the corner of Haile Selassie and Ali Hassan Mwinyi Roads, midway between the

the city centre and Msasani Peninsula. These fully furnished apartments are the outstanding value-for-money option in the city. They also have one of the best restaurants around. Tel: +255 22 2666665, e-mail: proteadar@africaonline.co.tz

Sea Cliff Hotel – Spectacular setting at the end of Msasani Peninsula. Tel: +255 22 2600444, e-mail: karen@encountertanzania.com

Coral Beach – Small boutique hotel on the seafront along Msasani Peninsula. Tel: +255 22 2601928, e-mail: info@coralbeach-tz.com

EATING OUT AND NIGHTLIFE

The Club Room – Understated setting at the Protea Hotel Oyster Bay belies the quality of fusion and Mediterranean cuisine.

Calabash – Continental cuisine at the Sea Cliff Hotel.

Oyster Bay Grill – Steaks and seafood at the Oyster Bay Hotel. Has a restaurant and separate bar area.

Adidas in Dar – Along Ursino Road in Regent Estate; offers fantastic Ethiopian food in traditional settings.

Sweat Eazy – In the Oyster Bay Shopping Centre; African and Thai food with bar and nightclub alongside. It's also a great lunchtime venue.

Garden Bistro – Set amongst lush gardens on Haile Selassie Road, this complex offers a choice of dining areas and bars, including a big-screen sports bar and pool tables.

Q Bar – Late night spot, off Haile Selassie Road in Oyster Bay; always has a great mix of locals and expats. Live bands perform over the weekends, and there are pool tables and plenty of TV screens for sports lovers.

SHOPPING

Mwenge Craft Market – The largest arts and crafts market in Dar, on Sam Nujoma Road, which is off Bagamoyo Road.

The Slipway – This shopping and accommodation complex overlooks Msasani Bay, and includes coffee shops, restaurants, clothing and craft stores and a large bookstore.

Sea Cliff Village – A few designer outlets and restaurants at the end of Msasani Peninsula.

City Centre – Ask to be directed to the Asian quarter to browse the mini-markets and material stores.

ARUSHA

Arusha, always bustling and busy, is the **fourth-largest** urban area in Tanzania, and reputed to be the fastest-growing one. Because of its proximity to many national parks in the north, it is also the centre of the safari tourism industry. For visitors heading to the Serengeti, Ngorongoro Crater, Lake Manyara and Tarangire, and for those doing extended hikes up Mt Meru, Arusha is likely to be the entry and exit hub. Safari options aside, and despite its scenic location beneath the shadows of Mt Meru and within clear sight of Mt Kilimanjaro, it's not a place one would choose to spend excess time. If you do happen to have a few nights in town though, there are some wonderful lodges amongst the forests on the outskirts, and a little exploration through the central streets will unearth some places of interest. When walking around Arusha though, be careful, as petty crime is common.

THINGS TO DO

German Boma/Via Via Cultural Centre – The old fort in the centre of town offers a glimpse of the region's early history and that of the German colonial period. Behind it is the Cultural Centre and café, which is where many of the upcoming artists and musicians hang out. There's always a programme of upcoming events available.

Arusha National Park – If you have a day to spare, this is a must-do day or half-day trip. The park entrance is about 40 kilometres outside of town on the Moshi Road. You can also book through one of the local operators or at your hotel.

Cultural Tours – There are a number of trips available to the surrounding villages. A visit to one of Ng'iresi, Ilkiding'a or Mulala will give interesting insight into the life of the local Meru people.

WHERE TO STAY

Rivertrees Country Inn – Country charm in a tranquil forest setting about 30 kilometres out of town on the Moshi road. It also has perfect views of both Mt Meru and Mt Kilimanjaro, and a great restaurant. Tel: +255 27 2553894, e-mail: rivertrees@habari.co.tz

Ngare Sero Mountain Lodge – For yoga lovers, Ngare Sero is the place to be: a converted old farm

house set amongst stunning forests and freshwater pools approximately 25 kilometres outside town on the Moshi road. Tel: +255 27 2553638, e-mail: reservations@ngare-sero-lodge.com

Arusha Hotel – With all the modern facilities and a number of restaurants, this is the best option for those who want to be in the centre of town. Tel: +255 27 2507777, e-mail: info@newarusha.com

Impala Hotel – This is a cheaper alternative to the Arusha Hotel, situated in the leafy suburbs. Tel: +255 27 2508448/49, e-mail: impala@cybernet.co.tz

EATING OUT AND NIGHTLIFE

The Patisserie – For daytime snacking; in Sokoine Road just down from the Arusha Hotel, and it has the best internet café in town.

Ciao Gelati – A coffee shop in the Shoprite Complex that also offers the only decent ice-cream in town. There are a number of other coffee shops and small restaurants in this complex.

The Greek Club – Offers pub fare for those wanting to watch all the international sport on television.

Impala Hotel – The best curries in town.

Khan's Barbeque – And now for something completely different; awesome Swahili barbequed chicken and condiments amidst the hustle and bustle of the back streets. Also affectionately known to its hardcore local devotees as Chicken on the Bonnet.

SHOPPING

Mt Meru Curios and Craft Market – In Fire Road about 400 metres from the Arusha Hotel, this is the best place for all your local arts, crafts and curios, plus the chance to mix with the local Maasai, Makonde and Meru vendors. There are various other smaller local markets around town.

Cultural Heritage – Possibly one of the largest and best-stocked arts, crafts and curios complexes found

Top: *An Arusha street scene.*
Middle: *For yoga lovers, Ngaro Sero Mountain Lodge in Arusha is the place to stay.*
Bottom: *Khan's Barbeque in Arusha offers fantastic Swahili food in a very local setting.*
Opposite left and right: *The twin faces of Nairobi: the impressive city skyline on the left, and, a mere 10 kilometres away, Kibera, regarded as one of the continent's most densely populated slums.*

anywhere in Africa, but be careful of prices. On the edge of town alongside the Arusha Airport road.

Swala Gem Traders – This is the most reliable and professional jeweller for tanzanite and other gems; situated in the Arusha Hotel.

Shoprite Complex – Large supermarket on the main road through town. Also has a collection of coffee shops and art and clothing stores, amongst others.

NAIROBI

Most visitors spend as little time as possible in **Kenya's capital city**, which is much maligned for its high crime rate and congestion. Yes, crime is an issue (locals refer to it as Nairobbery), and the main street traffic-circles are a nightmare, but the assessment may be a little harsh, as it is no worse than most other large African capitals. The high crime statistics come mostly from the surrounding shantytowns and some of the suburbs, and if you avoid these areas, and do not walk the streets after sunset, you may just warm to the place. It's also not a bad idea to avoid the rush hour traffic when moving in and out of the city.

Nairobi had its beginnings **back in 1899** as a railway siding for the Ugandan Railway at the Mile 327 marker. Railwaymen erected the first tin shelters on the banks of a stream, known then to the Maasai as Uso Nairobi (meaning cold water), surrounded by plains teeming with wildlife. The city only really became established once the British moved their headquarters here from Mombasa, and the railway line linking Uganda with Kenya was completed.

Like many African capitals, Nairobi is now a city of **major contrasts.** Glass skyscrapers and large office blocks tower over the nearby slums, and fashionably clad business-folk and hip students jostle for pavement space with unruly hawkers and beggars. Traffic flow in the city can be near chaos, as a mix of supermodern SUVs and saloons attempt to outmanoeuvre the constant crush of overloaded *matatus* (minibus taxis), trashed trucks, and rudimentary pushcarts. Plush hotels share their street addresses with all manner of less appealing lodgings. Consumerism flourishes in Nairobi, despite sluggish national economic growth statistics. Countless large shopping complexes and supermarkets in the suburbs vie for sales with bazaars and street vendors, and the city is packed with retail outlets selling everything from cheap electrical appliances to designer furniture and clothing.

The most popular attraction for the nature-conscious tourist is the David Sheldrick Wildlife Trust.

ANGELA SHELDRICK

If courageous and successful wildlife conservation in Kenya is the topic, the Sheldrick name will usually crop up at some stage. David Sheldrick, universally regarded as one of Kenya's most committed and visionary conservationists of his time, was the first warden of Tsavo National Park, and his wife Daphne has received worldwide recognition for her groundbreaking work in raising orphaned elephant and rhino before returning them to the wild. Inspired by her parents, Angela is set to follow in their celebrated footsteps. She is currently still working alongside Daphne, but will in time be taking over the reins of the David Sheldrick Wildlife Trust, a conservation body established in her father's memory. Since Daphne first established the trust, they have successfully raised 60 orphaned elephant, 14 black rhino, 33 buffalo and untold numbers of smaller species.

Passionate about the work and committed to conservation in Kenya, Angela has broadened the scope of the trust to include a number of crucial field projects that are undertaken in conjunction with the Kenya Wildlife Service. The headquarters in Nairobi National Park, including the popular visitors' centre, remains a focus for operations. Meanwhile intensive anti-poaching and de-snaring around Tsavo, the running of mobile veterinary clinics, and community outreach and education programmes are now integral to the success of the trust's vision.

Outside of these responsibilities, Angela still has time to pursue her second love, art, which she studied at Michaelis Art School at the University of Cape Town. Her work is done mostly on large canvases, and is inspired by the wildlife and the colours and textures found in the clothing, jewellery and homes of the local African people. It captures these characteristics in a vivid mix of oils and water colours. She has one exhibition to her credit and her work is in high demand on a commission basis.

THINGS TO DO

The David Sheldrick Wildlife Trust – Based in Nairobi National Park. A visit to this elephant and rhino orphanage is a must. Tel: +254 20 891996, e-mail: rc-h@africaonline.co.ke

Nairobi National Park – Bordering the outskirts of the city and suburbs, this park is easily accessible and makes for a worthwhile day trip.

National Museum – On Museum Hill Road just outside the city centre. Worth visiting for its natural history and cultural exhibits.

Ngong Racecourse – Fancy a day at the races? Head for East Africa's only professional horse-racing track.

The Giraffe Centre – An animal centre in Langata that offers the chance to get close to tame Rothschild's giraffe.

WHERE TO STAY

The Norfolk Hotel – Built in 1904, the capital's oldest hotel has been a favourite with a host of film stars, international politicians and royalty over the years. Within easy walking distance of the city centre. Tel: +254 20 250900, e-mail: norfolkgm@lonrhohotels.co.ke

The Stanley – Also steeped in history, this Victorian-styled establishment is in the city centre on the corner of Kimathi and Kenyatta Roads, and is a favourite with the business community. Tel: +254 20 228830, e-mail: gm@thestanley.sarova.com

Nairobi Serena Hotel – Arguably the best option, this large modern hotel is set amidst gardens on the edge of Central Park. It has a choice of restaurants. Tel: +254 20 2822000, e-mail: nairobi@serena.co.ke

Giraffe Manor – This double-storey family mansion built in Karen in the 1930s has a resident herd of Rothschild's giraffe, which are likely to join you for breakfast. There is an educational centre at the foot of the gardens. Tel: +254 20 891078, e-mail: giraffem@kenyaweb.com

House of Waine – Reasonably new on the Nairobi scene, this small and stylish boutique hotel is situated in the leafy suburb of Karen. Tel: +254 20 891820, e-mail: mail@houseofwaine.co.ke

EATING OUT AND NIGHTLIFE

Talisman – Restaurant in Ngong Road offering fantastic fusion food. Superb atmosphere with styling that has a hint of the Middle East.

The Carnivore – World famous for its huge selection of char-grilled meat dishes. Near Wilson Airport in Langata.

Misono – Just Japanese, and the very best in all of East Africa; in Hurlingham.

The Handy – Fabulous curries and Asian dishes in Westlands.

Tamarind Nairobi – The capital's finest seafood restaurant; situated in the National Bank Building in the city centre.

Nairobi Java House – A stylish coffee shop, deli and bakery in The Junction.

SHOPPING

Sarit Shopping Mall and **Yaya Mall** – Two of Nairobi's largest malls with a wide selection of shops, super-markets and eateries.

The Junction – A new centre with an eclectic mix of designer stores and craft shops; off Ngong Road.

The Village Market – Shop with the expats in Gigiri; designer shops, craft stores and restaurants.

The Westlands Market – A maze of a market selling the largest selection of local arts and crafts. Right alongside the Sarit Shopping Mall.

Art galleries – Art in a variety of forms is available throughout the city, but if you want the best, RaMoMA in Upper Hill specialises in the most celebrated Kenyan artists, or Gallery Watatu in the city centre and Tazama in Yaya Centre offer a wide selection of works.

Below left: *The morning call for residents at Giraffe Manor in Nairobi.* **Below right:** *Rush-hour traffic along Kenyatta Avenue in Nairobi.*

The Tanzanian coastline

There is plenty of Tanzanian coastline, 1 424 kilometres to be precise, but unlike the Kenyan coastline, it is mostly undeveloped and has few enticing beach settings. Besides a few spots north and south of Dar es Salaam, the offshore islands of Zanzibar, Pemba and Mafia are the beach destinations of choice in Tanzania.

SOUTH OF DAR

Although the short stretch of scenic coastline immediately south of Dar is extremely popular, most places are budget options. Take the Kivukoni Ferry from the centre of the city, and get beyond the villages of Kigamboni and Gezaulole to reach the two beach lodges worth considering.

Ras Kutani, set amongst coastal forest where a freshwater lagoon spills out into the warm azure waters of the Indian Ocean, ranks with the very best the offshore islands have to offer. Time here is best spent lazing on the soft sandy crescent-shaped beach in sloppy silks and faded cottons, and taking daily forest walks in search of colobus monkeys. Although rest and relaxation top the agenda at Ras Kutani, there is a range of water sports on offer for the more energetic.

On the next stretch of shoreline along the coast is the **Protea Amaani Beach**, a small boutique hotel hidden amongst expansive gardens.

NORTH OF DAR

This section of coast has substantially more development, focused around the historical town of Bagamoyo and the beaches stretching up to Pangani and Tanga. Between Dar and Bagamoyo, **Lazy Lagoon Island** is a pleasant beach stopover, but you can skip the multitude of popular but sterile resorts immediately north of the capital.

Next up is **Bagamoyo**, an ancient Swahili trading and slaving port. Despite its lyrical name and prominent place in the region's history books, this derelict and dirty fishing and dhow-building town has a somewhat forlorn feel to it. This may change though, as it does have a number of beach resorts. Since it is also less than an hour's drive north of Dar, companies based in the capital are increasingly finding it an appealing location for conferences.

Those interested in the life of Livingstone, in the slave trade (the name Bagamoyo means 'to lay down your heart' in reference to the despair of captured slaves as they were crammed on to slaving ships), and in Swahili history should find a visit worthwhile. There is also the Bagamoyo College of Art that is worth checking out. Try the Travellers Lodge for reasonably-priced chalets and camping, or the Millennium Sea Breeze Resort for something a little flashier.

Saadani National Park, one of two recently proclaimed parks, is a short distance north of Bagamoyo, and the classic 'bush meets beach' destination. A mix of acacia and dry woodland interspersed with scrub and grassland, the park carries reasonable populations of some of the plains game species, and occasionally lion and buffalo can be spotted. From the recently refurbished **Saadani Safari Lodge**, highlights include a slow cruise on the mangrove- and palm-lined Wami River, and of course, the experience of heading straight to the beach and into the ocean after your game drive.

Also worthy of mention is **The Tides**, a homely and intimate beach lodge south of Pangani. The expansive beach and an outstanding menu make this a fantastic value-for-money getaway, particularly for the Dar crowd.

Chilling on Ras Kutani beach, the best option on the mainland coast of Tanzania.

Catch of the day in Bagamoyo, northern Tanzania.

The Kenyan coastline

Prior to the boom in coastal tourism that took place from the late 1980s, Kenya's coast had earned itself a reputation as one Africa's most exotic and undiscovered destinations. Beach paradise was part of the lure, but combined with the laid-back tempo and mood of undeveloped coastal life, and Africa's unique style, the mix was irresistible to the more adventurous international set. But that image is now a distant memory as Kenya's coast has since been discovered in a big way.

Secluded enclaves still exist, but the general trend of development has turned to mass-market tourism aimed at the budget-conscious Europeans, particularly the stretch between Diani Beach and Malindi. Unless you want to share your vacation with the crowds, avoid Christmas, New Year and the peak European holiday periods.

Within the tourism industry, resorts and towns are known as being either North Coast or South Coast, depending which side of Mombasa they are located. Generally, the coast is scenic with some idyllic locations, but you should take care when choosing your spot in the surf and sand. Almost all destinations will offer fishing, diving, snorkelling and a variety of other water sports, and accommodation options range from private homes and boutique guesthouses and lodges to all-inclusive packages in large complexes with 200 or more rooms.

MOMBASA

Despite its historical significance, and its status as the country's **second largest city,** Mombasa could readily be left off a Kenyan itinerary. It's a grimy, muggy place that strains under the constant hustle and bustle typical of an overcrowded African city. It's Kenya's only major port, with its central regions situated on an island within a coastal inlet geographically suited for deep-water berthing. Mombasa is notable as the busiest cargo-handling harbour along the East African coastline, and because most visitors on a fly-in package holiday to the coastal resorts will have to pass through its international airport.

Those who are interested in its historical sites will find them in the Old Town section; they are best vis-ited as a day trip from the coastal resorts. Most are relics from Mombasa's heyday as a Swahili city-state, from the Portuguese period when it was the seat of the colonists' interests along the East African coastline, and finally from its role as a commercial and administrative hub under British colonial rule. **Fort Jesus**, a substantial structure built by the Portuguese in 1593, is the prize exhibit, and is worth at least a few hours. Follow Nkrumah Street to the seafront and the entrance to the Old Town harbour.

If you have to spend a night here, choose the **Tamarind Village** across Tudor Creek from the Old Town. It has the Tamarind restaurant, which offers an outstanding seafood menu with some delectable Swahili recipes. The group also has the Tamarind Dhow, which sets sail from the front of the village for lunchtime, sundowner or dinner trips around Tudor Creek.

THE SOUTH COAST

The South Coast stretches from Mombasa to the border with Tanzania, a distance of just under 100 kilometres. **Diani Beach** is the major resort town, with its fine bathing waters and powdery beaches attracting the highest percentage of Kenya's overseas visitors to the coast. As a result, the beachfront has been extensively developed with large hotel complexes and self-contained housing units, and the main feeder road behind these carries all the shopping and commercial outlets one expects from a hub. To avoid the throng, head for **Pinewood Village** on the south side of town, or **The Cove**, a responsibly developed treehouse resort with private beach and surrounding tropical forest. An added attraction is their **Shimba Hills National Park** retreat, the Ndovu Bonde Treehouse, which offers guests a two- or three-day safari package with the beach stay. For privacy, opt for **Diani House**, a large beachfront villa in spacious gardens.

Diani does have the most remarkable restaurant location along the coast. Set in a cavernous underground section of fossilised coral rock, **Ali Barbours Cave** (Tel: +254 127 3202033) offers diners a fantastic meal in exceptional surroundings. **Forty Thieves**

Top left: A beach scene in Malindi, Kenya.

Top right: The coastline around Watamu on Kenya's North Coast is dominated by these ancient coral outcrops.

Left: Camel rides along the beaches of Diani are a popular option with visitors.

Above: The Colobus Trust, a primate sanctuary in Diani, makes for a most worthwhile visit.

Next page: Fishing craft at anchor off the coast of Watamu, Kenya.

and **Nomads** are the liveliest beach bars, and fun places to while away the hot midday hours or toast the setting sun. Worthwhile excursions from Diani include a day trip to the Shimba Hills National Park (bookings can be made from any hotel or resort) and a visit to the local primate sanctuary, **The Colobus Trust** (Tel: +254 40 3203519 or e-mail: info@colobustrust.org)

The tiny village of **Shimoni** lies about 40 kilometres south of Diani, and is the last stop before the Tanzanian border. Although the coastline itself is not particularly appealing, visitors are drawn to the area for its bill-fishing and diving. The deep waters of the Pemba Channel, which pass between the mainland and Tanzania's Pemba Island, are regarded by many as Kenya's premier marlin and sailfish waters, particularly from November through to March. Normally, fishermen need head no more than 20 kilometres offshore, as it is at this distance that the billfish congregate, feeding along the spectacularly steep drop-offs of the Continental Shelf. Lying about two kilometres offshore from Shimoni is **Wasini Island**, and, a short dhow ride beyond its outer reefs, are Kisite Marine Park and Mpunguti Marine Reserve, which offer Kenya's best diving and snorkelling opportunities. Both sites are easily accessible and have a wide variety of coral and fish species. They offer remarkable opportunities for close-up underwater encounters with whale sharks. Other highlights include a number of dolphin species, green and hawksbill turtles, and humpback whales passing through on their migratory routes. There are many operators ferrying tourists — mostly day-trippers — to the pristine coral reefs, but the best bet is **Pilli Pipa Dhow Safari**. They have a dive school on Wasini Island, and offer thoroughly professional full- and half-day scuba-diving and snorkelling trips using a large and stately dhow as transport.

THE NORTH COAST

Immediately north of Mombasa are a number of resort towns — Nyali Beach, Bamburi Beach and Shanzu — which should all be avoided as they are tacky and overcrowded. Further north is **Watamu**, the most appealing location along the mainland coast. It's more scenic, the pace is less hectic, and the local villagers are more considerate towards one's privacy.

It also has its fair share of large hotels, but seems to have escaped the intensity of development that afflicts its neighbours. Perhaps it's just the striking layout of the coast, three separate coves broken by steep-sided coral outcrops, that gives it the impression of being less crowded. These limestone outcrops average between five and 12 metres in height, and some form independent islets. They arose after periods of warming during the Pleistocene period that resulted in an average drop in ocean levels of 15 metres or more.

Watamu is home to the world-famous fishing resort **Hemingway's**, but although it is conveniently located along the main beach strip, recent renovations have turned it into another large and rather sterile complex. Even so it remains, along with **Ocean Sports** next door, one of the choice bases for keen bill fishermen. However, **Man Friday**, on the south side of Watamu across the Mida Creek, is the pick here. Fronting onto the Watamu Marine Park, it's a peaceful spot with loads of private beachfront, and its funky original design only adds to the appeal.

Within the immediate vicinity of Watamu are a number of non-beach highlights that will break the monotony of sun and sand. The **Arabuko Sokoke Forest Reserve**, the largest remaining tract of indigenous coastal forest in East Africa, is a haven for birders, and harbours six critically endangered species. One of these, the Clarke's Weaver, is only to be found within the confines of this 420-square-kilometre reserve. Kenya's coastal forests, already decimated by human activities, are under constant threat, so every eco-tourism contribution goes some way towards protecting this region's biodiversity — another reason to visit. Between the forest and Watamu village lie the **Gedi Ruins**, one of the most impressive Swahili historical sites along the entire East African coast. Established during the 13th century, but only rediscovered by archeologists in the 1920s, the site consists of a complex of houses, palaces, tombs and mosques. An early-morning walk before most visitors arrive makes for a memorable experience. For reptile lovers, the **Bio-Ken Snake Farm**, which is also a research centre and anti-venom production unit, has the largest collection of snakes in East Africa. The centre also offers the most unusual of safari trips, the 'Big Five' Snake

Safari, which ventures into well-known parks and reserves in search of cobras, vipers, pythons, mambas and boomslang (snakes@africaonline.co.ke).

Further north, **Malindi** is the last of the resort towns. While the old historical Swahili part of town is fun to roam around, the rest has little to offer. The coast on either side of the town is over-developed with dozens of cluster-home complexes, none of which have much appeal. The only place worth heading for is **Himaya House**, a private and spacious family home centrally situated on the main beachfront with great ocean views.

Above: *Watamu is the most appealing location along the Kenyan mainland coast.*
Left: *A Watamu 'beach boy'.*
Opposite: *Kenya's coastline is an extremely popular destination for European travellers.*
Page 76: *Tuberculosis is still a life-threatening disease amongst impoverished communities in Kenya and Tanzania.*
Page 77: *A street scene on the outskirts of Kisumu, the largest city in western Kenya.*

Fishermen from the village of Saadani along Tanzania's northern coast clean their nets.

on SAFARI

It is simply not possible to get the most out of Kenya and Tanzania from a single safari. These are vast lands, particularly Kenya's northern districts, and the central, western and southern regions of Tanzania. The choice of destinations and lodges is endless. If you want to get the most out of your stay, don't set yourself a whirlwind itinerary; **plan with a return trip in mind**.

Most first-time fly-in visitors do a circuit, taking in a selection from Tanzania's well-known northern parks and reserves and Kenya's southern ones. These are unlikely to disappoint, but it is worth bearing in mind that the game viewing is as good, and at times, the overall experience is even better, in some of the lesser-known outlying wilderness areas. Tanzania has a number of wonderful choices in the west and central regions, and in Kenya, as much wildlife is found outside nationally protected areas as within them; so visitors should give equal consideration to private concessions, conservancies and the many group ranches that operate on the edge of national parks. What's more, these destinations often provide a more secluded experience and, because they are mostly privately funded, community-based initiatives, you

may be making a tangible contribution to **local conservation initiatives**. These operators are often pioneers of conservation and eco-tourism, and they provide a fantastic product; they need the support your 'tourist dollar' brings.

One should also take the 'numbers issue' into account before deciding on a final itinerary. Because of the high-volume tourism that occurs in certain parks and reserves of both countries, the **tented mobile safari option** is an extremely appealing one. Your stay in the Masai Mara, Serengeti and Lake Nakuru for example, is likely to be enhanced by choosing a private mobile camp during the peak periods. It's a more authentic experience, and should keep you away from the crowds for much of the time.

No matter what choices you make, a distinguishing feature of any East African safari will be the **cultural exposure** that is part and parcel of the experience. In many areas, the very same lands that carry the herds of wild animals are the traditional lands of people such as the Maasai and Samburu. A safari in East Africa is also a window into the customary lifestyles of these incredible people.

National parks and reserves

Because of different resource utilisation policies, Kenya and Tanzania have dissimilar wildlife management structures and land use categories. In Tanzania, in addition to photographic safaris, both 'citizen' and trophy hunting are widely practised, while in Kenya, trophy hunting was banned in 1978 because of irregularities within the industry.

Tanzania has approximately 28% of its land under some form of protection, and land use is divided into three major categories.

The 14 National Parks, two Marine Reserves and the Ngorongoro Conservation Area – which together comprise 5% of the land – are for photographic tourism only.

The 31 Game Reserves, which account for 15% of the land, are designated chiefly as tourist trophy hunting areas, although limited photographic tourism is allowed.

There are 38 Game Control Areas comprising 8% of the land, which are designated as hunting blocs managed in conjunction with communities for both 'citizen' and trophy hunting.

There are also numerous small forest reserves scattered around the country, and a number of Open Areas, which exist primarily as hunting blocs, but which have no gazetted protection status.

The management of these areas is carried out by three bodies, all of which fall under the ministry of National Resources and Tourism. Tanzania National Parks (TANAPA), a parastatal run by a Board of Trustees, is responsible for the national parks; The Wildlife Division (TWD), which is directly controlled by the ministry, is responsible for all game reserves and for regulating the hunting industry; and the Ngorongoro Conservation Area Authority (NCAA) is responsible for the management of the greater Ngorongoro Crater region.

MAJOR NATIONAL PARKS AND RESERVES OF TANZANIA

Arusha National Park	137 sq km
Gombe Stream National Park	52 sq km
Katavi National Park	4 471 sq km
Kilimanjaro National Park	756 sq km
Lake Manyara National Park	330 sq km
Mahale Mountains National Park	1 600 sq km
Mikumi National Park	3 230 sq km
Ngorongoro Conservation Area	8 300 sq km
Ruaha National Park	12 950 sq km
Rubondo National Park	240 sq km
Saadani National Park	1 148 sq km
Selous Game Reserve	48 000 sq km
Serengeti National Park	14 763 sq km
Tarangire National Park	2 600 sq km
Udzungwa Mountains National Park	1 900 sq km

Previous spread: *Lions are a major attraction in the Masai Mara.*
Opposite: *This landmark candelabra euphorbia appears at the beginning of the descent road into the Ngorongoro Crater.*
Above: *Tarangire National Park is well known for its large elephant population.*

Kenya boasts 54 national parks, reserves and sanctuaries that make up just over 10% of its total surface area. While this is a large number, many of them are small, isolated and suffer from poor management. Other than the Masai Mara, which is managed by various local county councils, all nationally protected areas are managed under a single body, the Kenya Wildlife Service (KWS). The country also has a number of privately-owned and -managed conservancies and community group ranches.

MAJOR NATIONAL PARKS AND RESERVES OF KENYA

Aberdare Ranges National Park	767 sq km
Amboseli National Park	392 sq km
Arabuko Sokoke Forest Reserve	417 sq km
Buffalo Springs National Reserve	131 sq km
Chyulu Hills National Park	650 sq km
Kakamega Forest National Reserve	240 sq km
Lake Nakuru National Park	188 sq km
Marsabit National Reserve	1 482 sq km
Masai Mara National Reserve	1 510 sq km
Meru National Park	870 sq km
Mount Kenya National Park	715 sq km
Nairobi National Park	117 sq km
Samburu National Reserve	104 sq km
Sibiloi National Park	1 570 sq km
Tsavo East National Park	11 747 sq km
Tsavo West National Park	9 065 sq km

Above: *Olive baboons in Lake Nakuru, Kenya.*
Below: *With Ol Donyo Wuas in the background, riders canter across the plains in the Chyulu Hills.*

Wildlife highlights

- East Africa has the **highest concentration of large mammals** found on any continent. The majority of this biomass is comprised of the approximately 1.5 million wildebeest, 350 000 gazelles and 200 000 zebra that roam the savannahs of the greater Serengeti/Mara ecosystem. For most visitors, the region's wildlife highlight is the **annual migration** that sees most of these animals moving in an annual cycle in search of better grazing conditions and water. Generally, they are in the Masai Mara from August through to October before moving towards the short grass plains in the south-east of the Serengeti once the rains begin falling. They calve here during late January and February, before moving north and westwards through the Western Corridor from March, where the rut takes place, and then back to the Mara.

- Although threatened outside protected areas, the **big cats** are regularly seen in most of the major national parks and reserves of Kenya and Tanzania. The Masai Mara, Tsavo, Serengeti, Ngorongoro Crater, Katavi and Selous are the best places to see lions, while Lake Manyara has a small population of tree-climbing lions. Cheetahs prefer more expansive savannah plains, with the Masai Mara and the Serengeti offering the best sightings. Leopards, though less often seen, are more widely distributed than the other large cats. Lake Nakuru, the Masai Mara, Samburu, Buffalo Springs, Serengeti, Selous and Ruaha all offer rewarding sightings.

- Tanzania has a population of about 1 500 wild **chimpanzees**, which can be seen at two national parks. The best place to view them is from Greystoke Camp in the Mahale Mountains, which are home to over 50% of the population. Gombe Stream has an isolated and far smaller population.

- During the 1970s and 1980s, poaching gangs almost wiped out East Africa's **rhino** populations. The black rhino's numbers in Tanzania fell from over 20 000 in the 1960s to a mere handful by the early 1990s. After a period of stabilisation, numbers are improving again, with Meru, Lewa Downs in Laikipia, Lake Nakuru and the Ngorongoro Crater the best places to see them.

- The drier northern regions of Kenya are home to a number of interesting species and subspecies. Amongst these are the **gerenuk**, an antelope with an extended neck, which feeds while standing on its hind legs, the **striped hyaena**, and the **Beisa oryx**. Grevy's zebra, with no more than 2 000 animals remaining, is an endangered species and one of Kenya's wildlife drawcards. The greater Laikipia, Samburu and Buffalo Springs regions carry over 50% of the total population.

- East Africa has a variety of distinctive **giraffe** subspecies. The most impressive is the reticulated giraffe, often seen in Samburu, Buffalo Springs and Laikipia in the north of Kenya. The most common species is the Masai giraffe, which occurs throughout southern Kenya and most of the savannah parks of Tanzania.

- The most impressive **elephant** sightings usually occur in the drier months when herds congregate at the dwindling water points. The best places to see them are Amboseli, Samburu, Buffalo Springs, Tsavo, Masai Mara, Katavi, Tarangire, Lake Manyara, Selous and Ruaha.

- **Wild dog** sightings are particularly rare in East Africa. The best chances are in the Selous, where an estimated population of over 1 000 dogs still occurs, and the Ruaha, which has a smaller but more regularly seen population. They may occasionally be seen in other reserves and parks.

- **Spotted hyaenas** can be seen in every national park or reserve. The Ngorongoro Crater, Serengeti and the Masai Mara have particularly conspicuous populations.

- The largest **buffalo** populations in Africa occur in the Selous (over 100 000). Other good areas include the Masai Mara, Amboseli, Katavi, Tarangire, Lake Manyara and Ruaha.

- The East African coastline has a number of **marine reserves** that usually offer excellent diving and snorkelling conditions. Reserves off the coastal towns of Watamu, Diani and Shimoni in Kenya, and the islands of Zanzibar, Pemba and Mnemba in Tanzania offer the best underwater experiences. The best sightings of the massive **whale sharks** are from Diani and Shimoni, while good **dolphin** sightings are made off Pemba and Zanzibar islands.

- East Africa has an immensely rich **avifauna**. Tanzania has a species list of 1 119 birds, which includes 34 endemics, and Kenya 1 080, with 11 endemics.
- Every wilderness area in the region offers a great birding experience. For **endemics**, the forested Usumbara, Uluguru and Udzungwa mountains in Tanzania are particularly rewarding, as are the lower lying forests of Arabuko-Sokoke and Kakamega in Kenya. The northern parks and reserves in Tanzania, and Kenya's dry northern districts offer the best savannah and woodland birding.
- For water birds, particularly **flamingos**, Lakes Nakuru, Bogoria and Baringo in Kenya, and Lakes Manyara, Eyasi and Natron in Tanzania are the best places. Rusinga Island in Lake Victoria offers easy access to large breeding colonies of cormorants and egrets. Because birds undergo seasonal movements, check with your operator before confirming a particular destination.

Right: *Sunset in the Serengeti.*
Below left: *From the front deck of the Ngorongoro Crater Lodge.*
Below right: *Tarangire National Park.*
Opposite: *More than 200 000 people visit the Ngorongoro Crater every year.*

In Tanzania

Tanzania's stock is on the way up. Having long languished in the shadow of its more developed and popular neighbour, it has over the last few years begun to attract attention from the safari world as a more authentic East African destination. Because it is substantially larger, distances are greater, but the end experiences most definitely make the travel time involved worthwhile.

THE NORTHERN CIRCUIT

The northern circuit comprises the most popular wildlife destinations. They are all within close proximity of each other and focused around Arusha, the town that serves as the safari capital of Tanzania. In a bygone era, the Serengeti, Ngorongoro Crater, Lake Manyara and Tarangire were all linked, forming what must have been an incredibly impressive and diverse mega-ecosystem. Today, though some migration between them does still occur, human development has created a degree of mutual isolation, and they are now visited as separate wilderness destinations.

THE SERENGETI AND NGORONGORO CRATER

Along with the Masai Mara in Kenya, these two wildlife meccas are the most widely known in East Africa, and would probably rank in the top five of most world wilderness lists. Blessed with masses of wild animals as they are, it is the distinctive ecological trademarks of each that enhance their status.

• The **Serengeti National Park**, a vast ecosystem of grassland plains and scattered woodlands peppered with granite outcrops, is the epitome of the African savannah landscape. For most visitors, it is the endless expanses of grassland that provide the lasting impression, although this is by no means the dominant vegetation type. It is no surprise, then, that the name Serengeti is derived from the Maasai word *siringet* meaning 'endless plains'. Eulogised by local tribesmen, early explorers and modern-day writers, poets and film-makers for its sense of sheer expansiveness and volume of wildlife, the Serengeti is now a World Heritage Site and listed as an International Biosphere Reserve. It also constitutes at least half of the almost 30 000 square kilometres that make up the greater Serengeti/Mara Ecosystem that also includes the Ngorongoro Conservation Area, the Maswa Game Reserve, and the Masai Mara National Reserve in southern Kenya.

• It is in this ecosystem where the **'great migration'** occurs, the single most impressive large mammal phenomenon on the planet. During the peak activity periods, it's an awesome spectacle of sights, sounds and smells with almost two million animals involved in an ongoing search for better grazing conditions. Almost 1.5 million wildebeest make up the bulk of the biomass, but they are accompanied at various times by 350 000 gazelles, 200 000 zebra, 12 000 eland and a profusion of other species, including the ever-present predators. Rather than a single seasonal phenomenon as many people incorrectly assume, the great migration is in fact an ongoing pattern of specific behavioural events, which, depending on rainfall cues, are instinctively played out in different sectors of the park. Covering anywhere up to 500 kilometres on their annual round

NGORONGORO CONSERVATION AREA CONDITIONS FOR VISITORS

1. Standing vegetation must not be damaged.
2. Fires must be lit in such a manner that they don't damage standing vegetation and that they don't spread; fires must be extinguished on departure.
3. No person may deposit litter any where in the conservation area.
4. All visitors must keep to the authorized roads and tracks.
5. All persons must remain in their vehicles within 200 metres of any wild animal.
6. All persons must obey the instructions of the conservator and his staff.
7. All visitors unless accompanied a licenced guide must take an official guide when entering the crater.
8. All visitors enter any part of the conservation area at their own risk.
9. Speed limit within the conservation area is 50 kph.
10. Speed limit in the crater floor is strictly 25 kph.
11. Off road driving in the crater is strictly prohibited.
12. All special campsites must be booked in advance.
13. No person may drive or travel in a vehicle in the crater other than a 4–Wheel vehicle.
14. Please read the information found behind your entry permit.

trip, these animals generally move in a clockwise direction from the short-grass plains around Ndutu in the southern Serengeti to their pre-calving stopover in the Masai Mara of Kenya, before moving south again.

• While there is a cyclical nature to the migration, it is still a natural and dynamic phenomenon. The exact numbers of animals involved, the month of activity and the precise location of the animals differs from year to year, and this has often frustrated safari visitors who may arrive full of expectation, yet miss the migration. Nevertheless, it is possible to give a rough indication of where to be during what months of the year.

• During the months from late January through to mid-April, the calving season takes place on the highly nutritious short grass plains in the south-eastern regions of the Serengeti. Over 300 000 young wildebeest are born, mostly within a three-week period once the rains have begun. Here **birth and death** occur on an epic scale. Despite the defensive advantages of the huge concentration of animals, the predators still get their fill and more.

• After the calving, the animals move westwards into the mix of woodland and red-oat grasslands of the Western Corridor, and along the Grumeti and Mbalageti Rivers. This is the dry season, and it is also the **annual rut** where tens of thousands of males noisily go about their mating duties. They are normally here from May through to July.

• As the short rains approach, the migration heads north over the Mara River and into the open grasslands of the Masai Mara. During this period there is much movement back and forth **across the Mara River** with thousands upon thousands of wildebeest seemingly unsure of their next move. Large crocodiles lie in wait and add to the mayhem. Visitors fortunate enough to see an attack will be treated to some high drama. It is not uncommon to see a large herd crossing one way in the morning, only to return in the afternoon. These crossings may occur any time from early August through to late November.

• Between the short rains and the long rains there is a short dry spell, and this is when the animals move southwards again through the acacia and commiphora woodlands that dominate in the northern and central regions of the Serengeti, before reaching the short grass plains for the **next calving season**.

• The incredible thing about the Serengeti is no matter what time of year you are visiting, it always offers fantastic game viewing. Plan with the spectacle in mind, but do also consider travelling to other regions, including the private concessions adjoining the park. Lodges such as **Kleins Camp**, **Migration Camp** and **Sayari Camp** in the north, and **Grumeti River Camp** in the Western Corridor are the best bets. For those wishing to camp, there are a number of sites throughout, although the majority are concentrated around Seronera in the central regions. And then there are the tented mobile camps, which are the best way to cover the calving in the south.

• The **Ngorongoro Conservation Area** (NCA), lying adjacent to the Serengeti on the park's south-eastern corner, was in fact once part of the original Serengeti National Park when it was first proclaimed in 1951. The local Maasai people, who had been forced from their traditional lands, campaigned and won the right to be included in the management plans of the region, leading to the establishment of the area's own body, the Ngorongoro Conservation Area Authority (NCAA).

• The crater's most distinctive feature, best viewed when approaching by air or from the upper rim, is the almost perfect condition and the awe-inspiring setting of its steep-sided 250-square-kilometre caldera. Sometimes referred to as the 'eighth wonder of the natural world', this ancient amphitheatre forms a unique haven for wildlife, with numerous habitats, including the alkaline Lake Magadi, a wetland and various woodland and grassland stretches on the floor. Over 20 000 large animals, including some of Tanzania's last remaining black rhino, thrive in these near-perfect conditions. The visitor merely needs to descend the crater wall in a vehicle; and once down in the bowl, viewing is almost effortless.

• Even easier is deciding where to stay. With its fabulous baroque styling and view-perfect location, the **Ngorongoro Crater Lodge** most definitely has pride of place here. Its distinctive décor and layout are not at all misplaced in this unique environment and guests can expect to be pampered throughout their stay.

Above: *Ngorongoro Crater Lodge offers its guests prime views across this world-renowned attraction.*

Next page: *Tarangire National Park has some of East Africa's largest and most impressive termite mounds.*

• Don't expect privacy in the crater though, as over 200 vehicles may enter during peak periods. The Conservation Area includes the adjacent range of volcanic mountains known as the **Crater Highlands**. This upland region has much to offer besides the wildlife. The archaeological sites in the Olduvai Gorge, often referred to as the 'Cradle of Mankind', make for a fascinating day trip. Bird walks into the dense forests on the outer slopes are always rewarding, and the chance to spend time with the Maasai people at the traditional *manyattas*, their corralled family settlements, completes a worthwhile few days.

LAKES MANYARA AND TARANGIRE

Lakes Manyara and Tarangire, both lying to the southeast of the Serengeti and Ngorongoro Crater, are often viewed by the itinerary writers as add-on destinations to their more famous northern neighbours. While they may not be as distinctive, they stand as fabulous options in their own right. Tarangire is a must for its wildlife, particularly during the dry season, and Manyara is home to Lake Manyara Tree Lodge, one of East Africa's finest safari lodges.

No matter from which direction one chooses to approach, **Lake Manyara National Park** always offers a pleasing prospect. From the Crater side, the spectacular drop from the Rift Valley escarpment gives amazing views across the ancient soda lake, and from Arusha, the same 600-metre-high wall of solid rock forms an imposing backdrop. Manyara is a small park, a mere 330 square kilometres, of which the lake occupies two thirds. Squeezed between lake shore and escarpment are a number of other habitat types; pockets of dense lowland forest, acacia woodland and stretches of open grassland, all watered by the streams that emerge from the escarpment. Because of the park's size, the large herds are not present, but game is generally plentiful, the birding is fantastic, and it is one of the very few places in Africa to see tree-climbing lions. Within the forests that encircle the main gate, the roadside baboon viewing is worth a day on its own.

On the far southern side, tucked in amid an enchanting mahogany forest, is **Lake Manyara Lodge**. Thoughtfully designed, beautifully built, and seductively private with all the quality service you can expect from a top safari lodge, it is a prime reason to include Manyara in your itinerary.

And now to 'the land of the giants', **Tarangire National Park**, dominated by elephants, baobab trees and some of the most gigantic termite mounds in existence. But there is so much more to this diverse and under-rated park, particularly during the dry season when herds of buffalo, zebra, giraffe and various antelope species are drawn in substantial numbers to what remains of the fast-diminishing water sources. During the wet season, much of the game disperses in a mini-migration to the outlying Game Controlled Areas, which make up the region's greater ecosystem. If you are travelling outside of peak seasons, there is still plenty to see, but with the added attraction of an environment transformed into a lush landscape of greens. Tarangire is also a must for keen birders, with the summer months being best.

The northern regions between the main gate and Tarangire Hill are the busiest, so it's best to head for **Swala Lodge,** a private tented camp in the remote south-western corner of the park.

THE WESTERN CIRCUIT – MAHALE AND KATAVI

This is Tanzania's remote west, a region still untouched by mass-market tourism and commercial development. Getting here is a long haul, even by charter flight, but well worth the detour, as these two gems are unique wilderness areas, and the experiences will most certainly be highlights of any safari trip.

The **Mahale Mountains National Park**, although appearing as a mere blip on Lake Tanganyika's sinewy eastern shoreline, runs for 50 kilometres along the water's edge and covers 1 600 square kilometres of substantial virgin forest. Comprising mostly lowland and montane species with tracts of miombo woodland and high-altitude grassland on the upper slopes, there are also remnant patches of West African tropical forest. Botanically speaking, it is an important region as it marks the transitional zone between the tropical rainforests to the west and the drier savannahs to the east. And it is here amongst this vegetative mosaic that approximately 800 to 1 000 **chimpanzees** belonging to one of three recognised subspecies, *Pan troglodytes schweinfurthii*, are found. By most counts, they represent over 50% of Tanzania's remaining chimp population, and although their conservation status is of concern, they are less threatened than the dwindling group that inhabits Gombe Stream National Park further north. This species was once found throughout these western forested regions, but intense human pressures, particularly from deforestation and illegal trafficking, have reduced their range and numbers to the extent that they are now classified as endangered.

It is a biological fact that we humans share more than 98% of our genetic make-up with the chimpanzee; well, nothing can prepare one for coming face to face with these incredible creatures, trying to figure out where the less than 2% difference lies. Tracking and spending time with one of the groups is what the Mahale experience is all about. The guides and researchers monitoring the chimps usually have a good idea of their movements, although they are not always successful in finding them; but once found, the two hours allowed with them will be among the most intriguing and rewarding wildlife encounters you can imagine. On the walks to and from the chimps, some of the eight other primate species found here may also be sighted. This makes for the highest primate count in any of the country's parks.

Although the chimps alone are sufficient reason to visit the lake, when you discover the delights of **Greystoke Mahale** camp, the full package becomes irresistible. Situated on the forest edge overlooking a sandy cove that breaks the lake shoreline, Greystoke is the very essence of the perfectly conceived East African safari camp. It simply has it all, and with the privacy that comes from being in Mahale, makes for the perfect hideaway. Dhow rides, lake snorkelling and bird walks, or merely lazing about on the beach, complement the morning hikes into the misty mountains.

Flying in a south-easterly direction over the Mahale Mountains, it's a short hop before one descends over the miombo treetops and across the flat savannah floodplains that mark the edge of **Katavi National Park**, the country's third largest. Apparently named after a legendary local hunter known as Katabi whose spirit is believed to endure in a particular tamarind tree, the park lies in the Rukwa rift valley between two escarpments, the Mlele Plateau in the east and the

Ufipa Plateau to the west. Much of the park effectively serves as a drainage basin for Lake Rukwa, which lies further south.

More than the country's other great parks and reserves, Katavi is very noticeably a place of two seasons; a wet and lushly green paradise over the summer period, it submits to the drier and cooler weather of the winter months, turning the landscapes into a harsher and almost unrecognisable palette of browns. But it is during this period that Katavi arguably ranks as the most comprehensive wildlife experience in Tanzania. Between the months of June and November, a substantial biomass, assembled from a rich diversity of species, congregates along the network of flood plains and river systems. Elephant, buffalo and zebra dominate, but some of the highlights include the masses of hippo noisily battling for position in the mud pools of the Katuma River, and the hibernation habits of the gigantic crocodiles. Although the wetter summer months are less active, the large herds are still around, and this is the most rewarding time for birders to tackle the park's species count of over 400.

Chada Katavi, a stylish camp hidden on a shady spit of acacia and tamarind trees overlooking Chada Plain, is the best place to be based.

THE SOUTHERN CIRCUIT – THE SELOUS AND RUAHA

So now you have seen the migration, been awed by the Crater and found the chimps. It's time to head south for something more remote and challenging. The Selous and Ruaha, like the western circuit, are wild and untrammelled, but much larger. This makes time spent here a particularly mind-expanding experience.

The **Selous Game Reserve** is the largest tract of protected wilderness in Africa. Bearing the name of the famous English explorer, Frederick Courteney Selous, it covers approximately 48 000 square kilometres, which is 6% of Tanzania's total land surface area.

Besides its inspiring size, the Selous has a number of other distinguishing features. It has never been settled in any way, other than by small pockets of people along its present boundaries. It remains East Africa's most pristine wilderness area. It holds the largest concentrations of hippo, crocodile, buffalo, elephant, wild dog and sable antelope in East Africa. It was

Above: *Stands of borassus palms are a feature of the waterways in the Selous Game Reserve.*
Next page: *Climbers on the Shire Route up Mt Kilimanjaro take a break to gaze up towards the summit.*

declared a World Heritage Site in 1982, making it the first ecological site in East Africa afforded this status; and in all probability, it was the first tract of wilderness in Africa to be declared a protected area.

As is the case with most of Africa's present-day parks and reserves, the first visitors to the area were the intrepid ivory and slave traders of the time. By the mid 1800s, caravans laden with valuable pickings were being driven from the interior and through the present-day reserve in order to reach the coastal ports. Explorers such as Burton and Speke (1857), and a number of European naturalists and artists soon followed in their footsteps. Protective measures began in 1896, when the then German governor declared hunting illegal in the areas north of the Rufiji River.

Selous first visited the region during the First World War as an officer in charge of a company of soldiers in pursuit of German troops. This followed a lengthy period spent in what was then Southern Rhodesia. Although he was an avid naturalist and hunter, he never managed to spend time here doing what he loved most, as he was killed in action by German forces in 1917. His gravesite can be seen today near Beho Beho in the northern regions of the park, which became formally known as the Selous Game Reserve from 1922.

The early conservationist promise has unfortunately not been fulfilled, and although more than a century has passed, over 90% of the reserve (all concessions south of the Rufiji River) is still controlled by trophy-hunting companies. The **Rufiji** carves its way in a broad brown meandering path across the Selous, forming the defining feature and the great divide between the photographic and hunting blocs. The Great Ruaha River adds its flow in the central plains. Beyond Stieglers Gorge, the system opens up as the river's force slackens, and, broken by large sand bars, becomes a network of channels and associated wetlands and lakes. This setting is unrivalled in East Africa for game viewing trips from motorised boats. The vegetation type is mixed; miombo and open woodland, savannah grassland, thickets and towering riverine forests of borassus palms fragmented by the river systems and rounded hillocks.

Factor in the impressive game concentrations, particularly over the dry season, and the bird species count of over 400 during the summer months, and you have the makings of a memorable safari. To get the maximum from the Selous, split your time between two lodges: **Sand Rivers Selous**, perfectly positioned on a rocky outcrop where the Rufiji extends into a broad sweep, offers a sublime waterfront option, and the recently revamped **Selous Safari Camp**, further north and overlooking the more tranquil waters of Lake Nzerakera, the perfect savannah complement.

Further inland is the **Ruaha National Park**, Tanzania's second largest. This and the Selous make an irresistible combination and the core of a regional circuit worthy of challenging the best of the northern parks and reserves. Centrally located within Tanzania, the Ruaha marks the overlap of the fauna and flora of Southern and East Africa. This brings a fascinating diversity, including, for example, the chance to see both the greater and lesser kudu, and both sable and roan antelope. The park also has many bird species on its list that do not extend further north or south.

If you are a wild dog enthusiast, then you must visit this park as it carries one of the continent's largest populations, and regular sightings are reported. Elephant and buffalo are also prime attractions, as are the herds of zebra and giraffe that concentrate along the course of the Great Ruaha River, the region's lifeblood.

Tucked away amidst a tranquil forest setting on the banks of one of the great river's many tributaries is **Jongomeru Camp**, one of Tanzania's very best. Stylish and elegant in the best safari traditions, this tented hideaway is the park's prime destination. A more affordable option, also with a fantastic river setting, is **Mwagusi Safari Camp**, a tented camp near the main gate to the park. Time spent in the remote and unblemished Ruaha is a wonderful getaway.

THE 'TWIN TOWERS' – MT KILIMANJARO AND MT MERU

If geographical features were ranked for the spectacle they offer, few would argue against Mt Kilimanjaro topping the African honours list. Rising in perfect isolation from the surrounding savannahs, this majestic mountain is **Africa's highest point** (5 896 metres) and the world's tallest freestanding mountain. On a clear day, the shimmering snow-capped upper slopes and glaciated peaks of Kili, as she is affectionately known by the locals, are visible from at least 150 kilometres away, and at its widest, the base stretches almost 60 kilometres along an east/west axis. A mere 45 kilometres to the west stands the more compact Mt Meru (4 566 metres), Kili's 'twin' tower. Guarding the bustling towns of Moshi and Arusha respectively, together these two volcanic massifs have a regional presence that dominates the northern landscapes.

MT KILIMANJARO

Lying three degrees or 330 kilometres south of the equator with its north-eastern flank abutting the Kenyan border, **Mt Kilimanjaro** is a relatively young volcano that appeared almost one million years ago through fractures in the Earth's crust associated with the formation of the Great Rift Valley. Before the weathering forces of nature played their role, Kili consisted of three magnificent cones. Shira, the oldest and most weathered of all, is on the western flank, and has been reduced to an extensive scree plateau supported by a ridge spanning its south-western edges, while Mawenzi on the eastern flank still remains reasonably intact with a peak of 5 149 metres. The glory belongs to Kibo, the central cone, which at approximately 500 000 years old, is also the youngest. Perched on the southern edge of the crater rim, its summit point Uhuru Peak is the Holy Grail of Kilimanjaro. Today, Kili is **classified as dormant**, with the last major eruption thought to have occurred over 100 000 years ago from Kibo. Minor eruptions have occurred as recently as 20 000 years ago, but over the last century, only sulphur emissions have been recorded.

While few of Kilimanjaro's geological features are in dispute, there is little consensus over the origins of its name. When the first explorers and missionaries began describing the mountain, some with poetic licence no doubt, they borrowed meanings and interpretations from Kiswahili and from the language of the Chagga people, the agriculturists who settled approximately 250 years ago around its slopes and on the sweeping plains beyond. The official Kilimanjaro booklet put out by Tanzania National Parks claims the name is most likely an amalgamation of the two words *kilima*, which is derived from the Kiswahili word *mlima*

for mountain, and *njaro*, which is said to derive from a Kichagga word meaning caravan, in reference to the 19th century trading caravans that would use the mountain as a stopover point. The word *njaro* is also reputed to have been used to describe a demon that caused cold conditions. Other texts refer to the word *kili* being a Kichagga one meaning lower limb, and *njaro* meaning loss or breakage, and together they refer to the manner in which early climbers and porters would succumb to the harsh conditions. Names such as the 'Shining Mountain' and 'Mountain of Greatness' are incorrectly put forward as translations for Kilimanjaro; these are instead more likely to come from the Maasai name Ol Donyo Naibor, meaning 'great white mountain'.

What is apparent in all these definitions is a sense of reverence for Kili, and along with its outstanding geological features, this has served to lure climbers of every ilk towards the summit. The first European accounts came from Johann Rebmann, a German missionary, who in 1849 wrote about a snow-capped mountain on the equator. It was not until 1889 that the first successful summit was recorded when Hans Meyer and Ludwig Purtscheller, two geologists, reached Uhuru Peak. Since then, untold numbers have been up, and today over 20 000 recreational climbers attempt the trip annually. It has been said that the climb 'can be summarised as a journey from the tropics to the poles'. Given the numerous vegetation changes that occur in altitudinal layers, this is a perfectly apt description. Once beyond the maze of cultivated fields on the lower slopes, the Kilimanjaro National Park boundary begins. From here, there are five distinct zones, each with characteristic vegetation and climate types. In general, one can work on lower rainfall and higher radiation when climbing, and a temperature drop of 1°C for every 200-metre rise in altitude.

• The lower slopes between 1 800 and 2 800 metres consist of dense **afro-montane forests** with a lush floor covering, which receives high rainfalls averaging 2 000 millimetres on the southern slopes and around 1 000 millimetres on the western and northern slopes. The common tree species include giant camphor, olive, fig, beech, yellowwood and cedar trees, some reaching over 40 metres in height. These

Mt Kilimanjaro is the highest free-standing mountain in the world, and at 5 896 m, Uhuru Peak is the highest point in Africa.

forests are where most of Kilimanjaro's wildlife may be seen, with blue monkeys, black-and-white colobus monkeys and a variety of duiker species being the most common. Over 40 bird species have been recorded, although the density of the forests can make birding difficult.

• Between 2 800 metres and 3 300 metres there is a narrow **zone of heather- and shrub-dominated vegetation**, particularly erica, everlasting and protea species. Rainfall is lower and temperatures are somewhat cooler, and there is often a cloud band hovering at these levels.

• Beyond this, and stretching up to 4 000 metres, is a dry and cool **zone of moorland,** which is dominated by tussock grasses and a number of peculiar endemic plant species including the tall lobelias and senecios. Specific highland bird species are still commonly seen, but animal sightings are unlikely.

• Between 4 000 metres and 5 000 metres the vegetation rapidly gives way to **alpine desert** where daily temperature variations range from below zero at night to warm balmy daytime conditions. Rainfall here is low (averaging 250 millimetres), radiation high, and snowfalls do occur at the upper limits. The dominant vegetation consists of lichens and mosses, although sparse coverings of tussock grasses and other moorland species do occur.

• The **summit zone** is characterised by extremely cold arctic conditions, with snow and glaciers dominating the barren rocky landscape. Rainfall here is less than 100 millimetres, radiation is extremely high, night-time temperatures fall well below zero, and oxygen levels are 50% lower than at sea level.

Currently, there are four popular routes to the summit, each offering alternative upper slope and descent options. Deciding on a particular route involves considering factors such as the length of stay on the mountain, and the degree of difficulty. There are a number of lesser known routes, including the Shira and Lemosho Routes, which begin on the far western flank and traverse the Shira Plateau, and the Rongai and Loitokitok Routes, which approach from Kenya and head up the northern slopes.

Machame Route – This route begins further west of Umbwe before cutting back across the edge of Shira Plateau towards Kibo. It is one of the longer routes, which allows for proper acclimatisation, and has spectacular views once you are clear of the forest zone.

Marangu Route – Because of its popularity, this is also often rather disparagingly referred to as the 'Coca-Cola run'. Traversing the south-eastern flanks of the mountain, Marangu is also regarded as one of the quickest and easiest routes, and almost 80% of climbers use it.

Mweka Route – Because of its steepness and the amount of scree, this direct route, which runs between the Umbwe and Marangu Routes, is the least appealing of the ascent options.

Umbwe Route – Ascending up the scenic southern slopes, Umbwe is the most direct route, and because it is fairly steep in places, is more suitable for experienced trekkers.

A word of caution – although climbing Kilimanjaro requires no technical mountaineering experience, it nevertheless remains a stern test by the elements, with high altitude and extreme cold conditions being the major challenges. For this reason, significant logistical planning, which includes acquiring the correct clothing and securing the services of experienced mountain guides, is crucial to a successful climb. Anyone wishing to attempt the climb should take the following steps:

• Consult your medical doctor regarding overall fitness levels and the risks of being exposed to high altitudes and extreme cold.

• Contact an experienced Kilimanjaro operator who will be able to match an appropriate route to your group and supply the necessary support and guides.

• It should also be borne in mind that not everyone reaches Uhuru Peak. There is no disgrace in turning back because of altitude sickness or fatigue, and this is always a preferable choice to exposing oneself to possible death.

Opposite, top: *Mt Meru, Tanzania's second highest mountain, is classified as a dormant volcano.*
Opposite, bottom: Lobelia deckenii, *an endemic moorland plant species found on the slopes of Mt Kilimanjaro.*

MT MERU

While for some **Mt Meru** will always be destined to stand in Kili's shadow, this should never be voiced to an Arusha citizen. Fiercely protective, they regard Meru as 'our mountain', and will always put forward a passionate argument for it in preference to Kili, the 'mountain in the distance'. And they certainly have a point. What it lacks in bragging rights in terms of height and glaciation is compensated for by **breathtaking scenery**, the populations of wildlife that occur on the mid- to lower slopes, and the best views possible of Mt Kilimanjaro. Along with the Momella Lakes and the Ngurdoto Crater on its eastern foothills, Meru forms part of the Arusha National Park, possibly the most under-rated park in all of Tanzania.

Tanzania's second-highest mountain is also classified as dormant, and lies across the Masai Steppe from Kilimanjaro. Meru is thought to have been formed millions of years before Kilimanjaro, possibly as long as 15 million years ago. Somewhere in its explosive past, the whole eastern half above 2 500 metres was blown away, giving the mountain its characteristic horseshoe shape. Inside the main crater is a smaller ash cone, formed by more recent volcanic activity, and above this and leading to the summit, some massive and spectacular steep-sided cliff faces. When viewed from Arusha, these impressive features of Meru are hidden by the solid western and southern faces of the mountain.

For climbers and hikers, Meru is more about basking in the splendour of the surroundings than overcoming the challenge, and with appreciably less human traffic than Kili, they have the freedom of the mountain. While there have been other routes in the past, the only one presently in use is the Momella Route, which begins at the Momella Gate of the Arusha National Park. It heads up through glades and glens, passing herds of grazing zebra and buffalo, across gleaming mountain streams and into the ever-changing forest habitats of the lower to mid-stratum slopes before cutting across and up onto the northern crater wall. Summit day sees the hikers walking the knife-edge between the spectacular cliffs of the inner wall and the drop-offs of the mountain's outer slopes. Meru can be conquered in three days, but four is a better bet for the average group, as that extra day for acclimatisation will improve the chances of a successful summit. And if you don't fancy the rigours of reaching the summit, the park is perfect for day trips and birding excursions, and some local operators offer canoeing and mountain bike trails around the lake system.

Although Meru is more than 1 000 metres lower than Kili, altitude sickness and cold conditions are still factors when challenging the mountain. One should **consult a reliable operator** and your medical doctor before heading out. And because of the wildlife, an added necessity on Meru will be an armed ranger as part of the guide group.

For avid hikers and climbers, there are a number of other mountain peaks and ranges worth considering. These include Ol Donyo Lengai, an active volcano sacred to the Maasai that is close to the Kenyan border, and the Usumbara, Pare, and Udzungwa Ranges, as well as the Southern Highlands and the Ngorongoro Highlands.

Bird watching along the Athi River from Kilalinda Lodge in Tsavo East.

In Kenya

Long the more favoured destination within the region, Kenya has over the last few years had to accept stiff competition from Tanzania's booming tourism industry. While it lacks, for the most part, the vast and remote wilderness areas that Tanzania boasts, for many it is a preferable option because it offers easier travel and a wider selection of lodgings.

As an alternative to the standard accommodations, Kenya Wildlife Service (KWS) offers a range of affordable self-catering options in many of the national parks and reserves. Known locally as *bandas*, they fill the niche between camping and the more expensive lodges and hotels. For enquiries and bookings, contact KWS. Tel: +254 20 607024/600800 ext 332 or e-mail: tourism@kws.org

THE MASAI MARA

Forming the northernmost wedge of the greater Serengeti/Mara Ecosystem, the **Masai Mara National Reserve** and the adjoining Loita Plains are Kenya's wilderness jewels. Even more than the Serengeti, the magnificent open grass plains, home to an abundance of wildlife, have been the flag-bearers of Africa's safari traditions. In wildlife circles there is not a film maker, travel writer, zoologist or photographer worthy of the name who has not 'done the Mara'.

Hemmed in by the Oloololo, or Siria Escarpment on the far west and the Ngama Hills on the east, and bisected by the Mara River into the Mara Triangle and the Central Plains, the region covers approximately 1 800 square kilometres. While there is always an astonishing collection of wildlife, the Mara is unsurpassed during the **peak migration period** from August to November when it is reputed to carry the densest concentration of large mammals on Earth. Arriving from the Western Corridor after the rut, the wildebeest and zebra will await the onset of the short rains here. The plains, blanketed with over 600 000 of these ungulates, somehow also have space for most other species including the unusual ones such as Coke's hartebeest and topi. This abundance of herbivores is a paradise for the large cats, especially lion and cheetah, as well as hyaena. They are never far from the action, and most visitors are likely to see some form of predatory performance from them. And if it's the life-and-death stuff you have come for, then the drama that unfolds at the river crossings should provide the thrills you crave. For it is at these crossings along the Mara, Talek and Sand Rivers that hundreds of large crocodiles lie in ambush, and as the thousands of wildebeest stampede into the churning waters, these ancient predators swing into deadly action.

These lands are also inextricably linked to the **Maasai**, the pastoralist Nilotic people who still uphold their traditional lifestyle on the numerous group ranches that fringe the reserve. In fact, the Mara sits almost centrally within the greater region known as Maasailand, which extends from Nairobi southwards through into Tanzania and beyond the southern extremities of the Serengeti. Many Maasai work as guides and lodge staff in the Mara, and for those visiting any of the group ranches, one is as likely to encounter Maasai herdsmen following their beloved cattle across the plains as a herd of wildebeest or zebra. And the association extends to the reserve's name, as the word *mara* is a Maasai one, meaning 'spotted' in reference to the mosaic of woodland and bush that scatter the plains. As always with human activity, the threat of encroachment and natural habitat loss is real. To counter this, the management practices of the reserve, applied by the Narok and Trans Mara County Councils, stipulate that a substantial portion of gate fees and royalty payments go to the local Maasai communities to entrench wildlife as the primary land use.

The Mara has countless lodging possibilities, so when making a choice, you will need to consider whether you want to be inside the reserve, on its boundary, or on one of the group ranches surrounding it. Each option comes with its own attractions – it depends, for example, on whether you want to be close to the migration crossings, to spend time with a Maasai family or do night drives. The choice that offers most options is **Bateleur Camp**, a luxury tented camp in the forested verge below the Siria Escarpment, on the boundary of the reserve.

Originality and style have long been trademarks of the Kenyan safari industry, and the much-féted **Shompole** is a fine example of both. Situated on a group ranch east of the Mara and within sight of Lake Natron over the border in Tanzania, Shompole has been described as a 'creation of imagination', and 'truly an unusual and exquisite place'. Partly owned by the local Maasai community, it has won numerous eco-tourism awards for the initiatives undertaken with its local partners. Innovatively constructed from various natural stone, thatch and woody materials, it has been celebrated in almost every top international magazine for its smooth, watery-white finishes, its lavish comfort and its tranquillity.

SOUTH-EASTERN KENYA – AMBOSELI, TSAVO AND THE CHYULU HILLS

Although only just over 100 kilometres to the south-east of the Mara, these three southern parks stand in stark contrast to the grass-filled plains of their well-trodden neighbour. The dry, dusty plains and pans of Amboseli are separated from the nearby dense woodland eco-systems of Tsavo in the east by the volcanic hills and mountain ranges that make up the Chyulus.

Small in size, but big on reputation, **Amboseli National Park** is, after the Mara, Kenya's next most visited wilderness. Two icons, the elephant and Mt Kilimanjaro, captured together in a single photographic image, have been mostly responsible for this. This image, of elephants grazing or gently padding along in single file with snow-capped Kili as the backdrop, has been the park's trademark for many a decade. So familiar is this scene that many believe Kilimanjaro to be part of Kenya.

Although it actually lies immediately across the border in Tanzania, the glorious mountain has nevertheless played a prominent role in structuring Amboseli's **stunning landscapes**. During the shifting and shaping of the Great Rift Valley that included Kilimanjaro's emergence, lava flows blocked off the surrounding drainage systems, creating the basin that makes up the greater Amboseli region of today. The lake, which once was deep, has been reduced to its present shallow levels after millennia of silting, and a deluge of volcanic dust and ash (Amboseli is a Maasai name

meaning 'salty dust') that settled after one of Kili's early eruptions.

Dry and dusty the plains may be, but they are not without ample wildlife, and water springs eternally here, as the melting snows of Kilimanjaro feed at least three wetlands year-round. The climate is perfect for the tree species that dominate, a variety of acacias, particularly the fever tree and umbrella thorn, which are further enduring symbols of the park. The prime wildlife sightings are the **continent's mellowest elephants**, well habituated to man after 20 years of intensive study by a team led by Cynthia Moss, while there are always chances of spotting lion and cheetah too.

Edging the largest of the acacia woodlands and with commanding views across to Mt Kilimanjaro, **Tortilis Camp** is where you should head. Away from the throng in the park's central regions, this luxury tented camp offers all the safari comforts. An added and exclusive bonus is the camp's game drive access to an adjoining private concession bordering Amboseli.

Blissful remoteness, as offered by the **Chyulu Hills**, can sometimes be more gratifying than lavish luxury and wild animals en masse. A narrow range comprising umpteen rounded volcanic cones linked by a series of ancient and more recent lava flows, the Chyulus incorporate the Chyulu Hills National Park and a number of Maasai-owned group ranches abutting its borders. The region's Moorish mountains and cropped grass plains are a haven for hikers and horse riders alike. Take to the hills on foot for a day, or mount up and spend time riding the fly camp route, and you may just find yourself extending your stay. While modest in scale, game sightings are everywhere, particularly wildebeest, zebra and hartebeest, and elephant are regular visitors to some of the waterholes.

Built half-way up the western slopes on a private concession, **Ol Donyo Wuas**, one of Kenya's highlights, is the epitome of the relaxed and welcoming lodge. With the most spacious and homely of chalets, and views of Mt Kilimanjaro from every angle including the swimming pool, it's not easy to resist the temptation to remain lodge-bound. If you find it hard to leave the lodge, do at least get out for a sunrise breakfast or a hilltop sundowner – the views alone are worth the effort.

Left: *The multi-branched doum palm is found throughout East Africa.*
Right: *Sundowners at Elsa's Kopje in Meru National Park.*

The **Tsavo National Parks** are Kenya's largest, and after the Mara and Amboseli, the most popular. This no doubt has much to do with their accessibility; the main Nairobi-Mombasa highway splits the two parks, and they lie within close proximity of the bustling coastal towns of southern Kenya. For many, the name of Tsavo will be associated with its legendary maneless man-eaters, the two lions that spread fear and mayhem amongst the community of rail workers constructing the Uganda Railway during the early 1900s. Administered as two separate units, Tsavo East covering 11 747 square kilometres and Tsavo West 9 065 square kilometres, together they comprise almost 40% of Kenya's nationally protected land and 3.5% of the country's total area.

Tsavo is at its most rewarding when visited during the dry winter months. The variety of biomes found in the parks makes them some of East Africa's leading biodiversity strongholds, but the general vegetation density makes game viewing outside of this period something of a mission. In season, with the largest herd in Kenya, elephants are the major attraction, and Tsavo is a prime spot for lions, although the man-eating variety is long gone. The plains game species are plentiful, and for those visiting during the wetter summer months, there is always the spectacular scenery of the volcanic lava flows and caves, and the Yatta Escarpment fringing Tsavo East.

Kilalinda, on a private concession adjoining Tsavo East and overlooking the Athi River, and **Finch Hattons in Tsavo West**, a luxurious throw-back to the Colonial Era, are the lodges of choice.

MERU NATIONAL PARK

'Back from the brink' is the only way to describe the recent history of **Meru National Park**. What was, until the late 1980s, a thriving tract of wilderness and one of Kenya's most popular destinations, was within a decade virtually lost to the world of conservation and tourism.

Under the spears and guns of the Somali poaching gangs and bandits, the wildlife populations were decimated. A seemingly hopeless situation was eventually turned around in 2000 after the appointment of **Mark Jenkins** (see box on page 104) as Head Warden. With the support of Kenya Wildlife Service, international donor funding was secured, which enabled them to tackle the poaching gangs and begin a restoration process. This included a reintroduction programme that saw over 20 white rhino, 20 black rhino, 500 Burchells zebra, 72 reticulated giraffe and 57 elephant brought in, along with a number of other species. It's now an ongoing initiative that should see the reserve fully restored as the premier northern park within the next few years.

The Meru Conservation Area comprises four protected zones totalling 5 300 square kilometres, and with its impressive size and diverse range of habitats, including a variety of savannah and woodland ecosystems, palm and riverine forests and wetlands, it is a substantial asset to Kenya's wilderness portfolio.

While the game may not be as prolific or as habituated as in the southern parks, Meru still offers good sightings of rhino, buffalo and a variety of the plains game species. For birders, it's a prime destination with a species list of over 350, many of which are East African endemics.

Elsa's Kopje is the pick of Meru's lodges. It is named after Elsa the lioness, made famous by George and Joy Adamson in the film 'Born Free'. Built around Mughwango Hill above where the Adamsons built their original camp, it has all the comfort, style and privacy that is the hallmark of privately owned Kenyan lodges. The panoramic views onto the surrounding plains and the Nyambene Mountains help make Elsa's a place of peace and tranquility. A more rustic and economical option would be the comfortable self-catering bandas down on the banks of the Kiolo Sand River, which can be booked through KWS.

MARK JENKINS

The **Jenkins Family** has a long and illustrious association with Meru National Park. It all began back in 1968, the year after Meru was upgraded to national park status, when Peter Jenkins, Mark's father, was appointed the first Senior Warden. Through three stints covering 16 years, he established the park as one of Kenya's finest. And Mark spent most of his childhood here, growing up in the farmhouse a short distance from the headquarters established by his father.

Peter Jenkins retired in 1991, and Mark moved off to start a career in wildlife management. His first years were with the Kenya Wildlife Service (KWS) before he moved to South Africa to spend time working in the game capture industry. Spells in South Africa, at Murchison Falls National Park in Uganda, and in the vast undeveloped Niassa Reserve in northern Mozambique followed.

In the meantime, the Somali poaching gangs had moved in to Meru, claiming the land pretty much as their domain. Within a few years they had wiped out approximately 70% of the wildlife, and reduced tourism to a trickle. With Meru on the verge of being lost as a wilderness area and as a viable tourism destination, the turnaround began in 1999 when Mark returned, with his wife Clare and their children, to follow in his father's footsteps as Senior Warden.

His achievements to date have been remarkable. Living in his childhood home, which he renovated after finding it trashed and abandoned on his return, Mark and his KWS staff have within six years routed the poachers, re-established the park's infrastructure, and launched a large-scale animal reintroduction programme. Tourists are now returning to one of Kenya's premier wildlife reserves.

LAIKIPIA

The **Laikipia region** in northern Kenya comprises a collection of privately and communally owned and managed wildlife conservancies and safari lodges, and on the outskirts, cattle ranches and wheat farms. Stretching down from the foothills of Mount Kenya and across the Laikipia Plateau to the drier and lower lying acacia scrub plains beyond, this is some of Kenya's finest wildlife country, and one of Africa's most successful co-operative conservation initiatives. Coming together under the Laikipia Wildlife Forum and the **Lewa Wildlife Conservancy,** the stakeholders include landowners, scientists and researchers, traditional Maasai, Samburu, Borana and Turkana communities and various government departments. With the conservation of the greater ecosystem and its wild plants and

Top: *Cormorant and heron colonies on Lake Victoria.*
Left: *A lone Jackson's hartebeest on the plains of Lewa Downs in the Laikipia District.*

animals as the primary focus, these groups are actively involved in low-volume safari tourism, education and health care programmes, and improving the overall socio-economic standards of the region's people in order to secure this goal.

For visitors to Laikipia, there is a full safari schedule of activities and sights on offer. The region's free-roaming wildlife, which occupies over two million acres and a variety of habitats, includes some of Kenya's most endangered and unique species. The regular ones are all here, and Grevy's zebra and reticulated giraffe are a near certainty. Black and white rhino and gerenuk are commonly seen, and with a little luck, the striped hyaena and Lelwel's hartebeest may present themselves.

Laikipia has a number of Kenya's best-known lodges within its boundaries, many of them owned and run by third- and fourth-generation Kenyan families. A safari here is as much about gaining an insight into the life and times of their Anglo-African heritage as it is about having a wonderful time. **Borana Lodge**, perched atop a steep-sided ridge above the Samangua Valley, offers luxurious accommodation and one of the best horse-riding experiences. **Loisaba**, towards the western boundary of Laikipia, offers a variety of options from private farmhouse accommodation, through tented camps, to the main lodge, which offers sensational views across the plateau towards Mt Kenya. **Lewa Downs**, also offering a variety of lodge and camp-site options, covers a vast stretch on the north-eastern boundary below the foothills of Mt Kenya. This privately-run conservancy in many respects leads the way in terms of its conservation principles and the invaluable work it carries out in partnership with local Maasai and Samburu communities.

THE GREAT RIFT VALLEY AND WESTWARDS
Dominated by the towering mountain ranges and the lakes that define the Great Rift Valley, this region stretches westwards from Nairobi in central Kenya, through the scenic tea estates and down to the shores of **Lake Victoria.** Fertile and well watered, the country-side comprises some of Kenya's best agricultural land, which also makes the greater region the most densely populated in Kenya. While this is not classic wildlife country, those on road trips will find the routes that wind their way up and over passes and through the rolling country tea estates, particularly around Kericho and Kisii, some of the most pleasing in the country.

First up when heading west on the main Nairobi/Nakuru road is **Lake Naivasha**. Hemmed in by the Mau Escarpment on the west and the rift wall on the east, this is the highest of the large lakes (1 910 metres), and one of two freshwater ones in the Gregory Rift. Because of its proximity to the capital, Naivasha has long been a favoured weekend haunt for the Nairobi set. But that appeal may just be fading, as the lake-shore has, over the last decade, become the centre of the booming cut-flower industry. The area is now littered with hot-houses and industrial developments and already has a distinctly urban feel to it. As the industry continues to expand, so too will the plastic and concrete.

Of the many private estates and lodgings, the 243-hectare **Hippo Point** conservancy on the far western shores is noteworthy. Consisting of a stately English country manor house complex and Dodo's Tower, which has to be East Africa's most extraordin-ary lodging, it is set amongst sprawling gardens and an extensive fever-tree forest. Everything about Hippo Point is of the finest, making it a great place to relax at the end of a safari or to use as a base if undertaking a lengthy itinerary. Architecture and design enthusiasts in particular will feel truly at home here.

The pick of the parks is **Lake Nakuru National Park**, a tiny soda lake situated right on the outskirts of Nakuru, Kenya's fourth-largest town. Although a mere 188 square kilometres in size, which comprises mostly the lake itself, the park carries a diversity and biomass beyond imagination. First and foremost, it's a birder's paradise, with the flocks of flamingos and pelicans the main drawcard. Good seasons offer an unforget-table spectacle, as over one million lesser flamingos and a few hundred thousand greater flamingos flock to Nakuru's shallow saline waters to feed. Hugging mostly the northern, western and southern shorelines, the birds move about in a shimmering mass of pink, sifting the waters for the algal species that comprise their primary food source. Kenya's largest gathering of pelicans, with both the white and the pink-backed

Lake Bogoria is well known for its geysers and hot springs.

species represented, can be found on the water's edge near the main gate.

The acacia woodlands and patches of open grassland edging the lake offer Kenya's best rhino viewing, and leopard sightings are extremely common. Because it's a small park that is often crowded, the best way to experience Nakuru is with a tented mobile operator using the private campsites.

In the hot and low-lying regions further north, **Lake Bogoria** is famed for the dramatic rift backdrop that frames its prominent geysers and hot springs at a number of places along the lake shore. These boiling water seeps are associated with subterranean volcanic activity. Spurting plumes of steam create the warm-water conditions that provide the ideal breeding grounds for blue-green algae. This rich food source, at times so dense as to turn the lake's water bluish-green, in turn attracts the masses of flamingos that concentrate around the seeps. **Lake Baringo**, north of Bogoria, is the second of the freshwater lakes found in the Gregory Rift, and was once thought by colonial explorers to be the source of the White Nile. While it still has a high bird species count, the lake suffers mounting

environmental problems from silting and turgidity build-up. **Lake Magadi**, with its thick, crusted surface, is the most alkaline of all the lakes, and also the most southerly of Kenya's Rift Valley lakes.

Kenya's south-western corner is dominated by **Lake Victoria**, the largest of Africa's great lakes, and the second largest body of freshwater on earth. Although Kenya's rivers provide the majority of its waters, the country lays claim to only approximately 10% of its 69 000 square kilometres of surface area, with Tanzania and Uganda claiming the rest.

The shores are dominated by the Luo people, Kenya's second largest group. The lakeshores carry high population densities, with most locals scraping a living together from fishing and pastoralist activities. Kisumu, Kenya's third-largest city and the region's capital, sits on the shores of the lake. Although it is at present quite a sleepy place, this may all change, as the port facilities are likely to become central to trade with the revival of the East African Community agreement.

The best way to explore the lake is from **Rusinga Island Lodge**, a place of peace and beauty on the shores of Rusinga Island, one of many small islands

that dot the lake's waters. It offers all the water sport options, village tours, day trips into the Masai Mara and, with a number of incredible cormorant and egret colonies nearby, one of the best birding destinations.

Speaking of birders, the **Kakamega Forest Reserve** and **Mt Elgon National Park** are both immensely rewarding destinations worthy of a detour. The isolated rainforests of Kakamega, fast disappearing because of human pressures, contain a number of endemics, and the montane forests at the foothills of Elgon are at the very outer range of certain West African species. The national park is also well known for its elephant population, prone to digging for mineral salts at many sites, and has numerous fantastic hiking trails.

SAMBURU AND BEYOND

This is Kenya's rugged and remote country, and also its **most enthralling**. The wildlife is surprisingly bountiful, the cultural diversity rich, and the landscapes hauntingly beautiful. Still referred to by locals as the Northern Frontier, a name that is a relic from the colonial era, the region encompasses the dry lands of the three adjoining national reserves, **Samburu, Buffalo Springs and Shaba,** and then up through the Mathews Range and beyond to the semi-desert regions that include **Lake Turkana** (see Out of the Way, page 163) and the seldom-visited parks of Sibiloi and Marsabit.

Before rushing out, road-travellers should be aware that the regions to the north of Samburu and east of Lake Turkana have endured a troubled past at the hands of Somali bandits. For decades they were known as no-go areas; the strife has all but come to an end, but it is still advisable to check with local operators before venturing out.

The jewels are the three reserves just north of Isiolo. Strung out along the meandering Ewaso Ngiro River, the region's vital force, they hold a number of species not seen in the southern parks, and the outskirts are home to many ethnic groups, most notably the Samburu people. Mostly semi-arid lands, they are dominated by scrub and scattered woodland burnt brown during the dry months, yet transformed by the scant rains and the surging waters that flow during the wet season. Samburu on the northern bank and Buffalo Springs on the southern bank form a contiguous wilderness, and together are the more popular destination. Shaba to the east is less travelled, and notorious for the murder of Joy Adamson in 1980. The wildlife highlights include the range of species peculiar to these dry conditions – Grevy's zebra, gerenuk, reticulated giraffe and Beisa oryx. Elephant are common and visitors are likely to encounter at least one of the cat species.

Lodge seekers should stick to Samburu or Buffalo Springs, but for road travellers and campers, Shaba is a better option as you are likely to have the reserve pretty much to yourself. **Bedouin Camp**, another of Kenya's unique lodges, is found on a private concession bordering Samburu close to the West Gate. The fresh crossover styling, North African designs melded with East African fittings, is striking and blends perfectly with the oasis-like surroundings.

Further north, Marsabit, the forested mountain reserve that springs from the surrounding desert, and Sibiloi, the archaeological site on the far north-eastern shores of Lake Turkana, are somewhat off the safari circuit. Neither has much infrastructure, and they are best suited for adventurous road travellers or for booking with operators who specialise in providing tented mobile rigs in the region. (Rob and William Carr-Hartley Safaris; e-mail: rc-h@africaonline.co.ke)

MT KENYA

When you approach Mt Kenya (5 199 metres) by road, its understated profile – a distant and dwarfish-looking peak complex dominated by a massively broad base – belies its status as the **highest point in Kenya** and the second highest in Africa. Known as Kirinyaga, meaning 'place of light' to the local Kikuyu people, it is a place they have long respected. Only gods reside in such dramatic surroundings, and it is believed that theirs, Ngai, commands the scree-strewn valleys and rugged peaks. In honour of Ngai, all Kikuyu homes built within sight of the mountain are expected to face toward it.

Opposite: *A Samburu guide based at Bedouin Camp alongside Samburu National Park.*

Left: *This group of bull elephants become resident around Bedouin Camp during the dry season.*
Opposite: *A Samburu maiden.*
Pages 112–113: *The unique and distinctive style of the rooms at Ngorongoro Crater Lodge.*
Pages 114–115: *A 'tent with a view' at Bedouin Camp alongside Samburu National Park.*
Page 116: *On a game drive in the Masai Mara.*

Formed as a volcano possibly as many as five million years ago, Mt Kenya is now extinct, with its last eruptions having occurred between two and three million years ago. With the aeons of weathering, the crater walls have crumbled, leaving the solid volcanic plug that carries the mountain's jagged summit, the **twin peaks** of Batian (5 199 metres) and Nelion (5 188 metres). Below these snow- and ice-capped peaks are at least 10 glaciers, and since the mountain is situated a mere 16 kilometres from the equator, the peaks hold the distinction of being the truest equatorial ice-caps. A stretch of moorland lies below the alpine desert, followed by a heather zone, before the montane forests of the lower slopes, dominated by rosewood trees, give way to the rainforests and dry upland forests at the foothills. A peculiarity of the southern and western slopes is the dense stands of bamboo that occur.

After Kilimanjaro, Mt Kenya is the most popular challenge for climbers and hikers in East Africa, but there is one major distinction between the two; you need **technical mountaineering experience** to scale Mt Kenya's summit, while this is not necessary for Kili. In the past, Mt Kenya has incorrectly been viewed as an easier option than Kilimanjaro. The summit peaks of Batian and Nelion, while not as high as those of Kili, are technical climbs, which require ice-climbing experience and the use of ropes. They should not be tackled by inexperienced climbers. If in doubt, take the easier option and head only as far as Point Lenana (4 985 metres), the third highest peak. There are three major routes to Point Lenana; Naro Moru, the least demanding and most popular, and the two slightly longer and more strenuous routes of Sirimon and Chogoria. Because of altitude sickness and the cold conditions, you should consult your medical doctor, and contact an established operator when organising any excursion on the mountain.

For bookings and a base, the **Naro Moru River Lodge**, set amongst large and lush gardens on the foothills, is the best option. While some may find the old country feel a touch jaded, a complete equipment-hire store and the resident experienced mountain guides are the clincher. They offer a variety of climbing and hiking choices with full back-up service. Tel: +254 62 622126/2023 or e-mail: alliance@africaonline.co.ke

Kenya has a number of other options for climbers and hikers. Mt Elgon (4 301 metres), an extinct volcano in the far west on the border with Uganda, presents it own weather-related challenges, while the non-volcanic ranges of the Aberdares (4 001 metres) in central Kenya, the Chyulu Hills in southern Kenya, and the Cherangani Hills (3 529 metres), approximately 300 kilometres north-west of Nairobi, offer endless hiking trails into the moorlands.

Climbers and hikers in all these ranges will need to take altitude sickness and extreme weather changes into consideration. It is advisable to contact a reliable operator before heading out on a climb or hike. For further information, contact **The Mountain Club of Kenya.** Tel +254 20 602330, e-mail: mckenya@iname.com or website: www.mck.or.ke

Be guided

While location, comfort levels and the quality of attractions all go to making for a memorable safari, your guide will make all the difference between an ordinary safari and one of a lifetime. Because East Africa has a well-established industry, the region has a host of quality and experienced guides. Ask friends who have travelled to the region, or your agent, to recommend a guide who will fit your particular interests and type of safari.

Thomas Meela »

Thomas is in a small and select group of experienced Tanzanian mountain guides; he has reached Uhuru Peak, the summit of Mt Kilimanjaro, on over 500 occasions. Born in Marangu Village on the slopes of Kilimanjaro, where he still lives today on a small farm, he had the summit in his sights from as far back as he can remember. In 1978, and at only 16 years of age, he undertook his first climb as a porter for National Parks. Overawed by the experience, and particularly the spectacle of the massive glaciers, he vowed to make the mountain a life time's commitment. His first summit was in 1982 as an assistant guide, and he became a senior guide the very next year. In his words, 'My work is my hobby. I do not want to do anything else in my life.' Those who know him well attest to his calmness on the mountain, and his uncanny ability to 'read the physical condition of every climber in his group'. Despite his phenomenal achievements, Thomas has no plans of packing away his hiking boots. The mountain and its every mood is so entrenched in his soul that he dreads the day he will start his last climb.

« Richard Knocker

While Richard was born on a farm in Kenya, it's been in Tanzania that he has made his mark as an outstanding safari guide. After a stint studying English in the UK and leading expeditions in Turkey and safaris in the Masai Mara, Kenya, Richard and his wife Jules moved to Tanzania in 1994. They first spent time in Tarangire, and then, drawn by the extent of the wilderness, they moved to the Serengeti where they managed a camp. It was here that he gained much of his knowledge and experience of the vast ecosystem and introduced his trademark walking trips in the surrounding areas.

He is now well settled with Nomad Tanzania, spearheading their community conservation efforts in northern Tanzania, as well as engaging in conservation issues at all levels. He is also actively involved in the company's guide training programme

Richard's passion for the bush life remains undimmed and he revels in the opportunity to introduce like-minded enthusiasts to the joys of the African wilderness.

Ludovic Saronga (right) »

Having spent almost his entire 13-year guiding career based at Selous Safari Camp in the Selous Game Reserve, Ludovic knows the mosaic of woodland and lakes that dominate the terrain north of the Rufiji River better than most. A life in the wilderness became Ludovic's ambition from an early age. Born and brought up in Moshi below Mt Kilimanjaro, his family home was right alongside the Mweka College of Wildlife. His dream to join the college materialised after leaving school when he attained a Diploma in Wildlife Management. He added further diplomas in tourism management and hotel operations and studied on various guide training courses before settling in the Selous. For him, the magic of the place lies in the vastness of the wilderness and the variety of activities allowed. For Ludovic the most rewarding moments are when on foot explaining the finer points of the environment to his guests. His favourite month is September just before the hot and dry period sets in as 'this is when the bush and the animals are at their peak'.

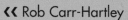

« Rob Carr-Hartley

The Carr-Hartley Family is synonymous with almost every aspect of East Africa's wildlife industry. Now fourth generation in Kenya, Rob, along with his brother William, continue the legacy under the banner of Robert and William Carr-Hartley Safaris. Born and brought up on Rumaruti Ranch in the Laikipia district, Rob's first experiences were more Hollywood than hunter, as the family ranch was the primary location for many of the early African-themed feature films shot on the continent. After 24 years of guiding throughout the region, his operation is now firmly established as one of Kenya's premier luxury tented mobile operations. Rob is also a renowned photographer, having won Kenya's Photographer of the Year award on four occasions. He is particularly well known for his work on the Maasai and Samburu people. Rob's other interests include flying – he has both a private pilot's and helicopter license, and conservation. He has sat on the Board of Trustees for Kenya Wildlife Services and is actively involved in The David Sheldrick Wildlife Trust as a trustee and field advisor.

Peter Kiyaa and Daniel Olekasoo »

From the same Maasai peer group in the village of Il Ngwesi bordering Samburu National Park, Peter and Daniel have trodden similar paths to becoming the senior guides at Lewa Safari Camp in Laikipia. Peter was inspired by his uncle, who took a position as a game scout in the Lewa Wildlife Conservancy, and Daniel stumbled across the opportunity when taking a colleague for an interview at the same conservancy. Both began doing anti-poaching work, and because of their commitment and tracking skills, they were soon chosen to undergo full guide training. Peter has undertaken numerous courses and diplomas and he wants to complete a degree in wildlife management. Daniel has his ambitions set on marketing, particularly the community lodges established in conjunction with the Lewa Wildlife Conservancy in Laikipia. Outside of guiding, they participate in community projects run by Lewa, and Peter is assistant manager at Lewa Safari Camp. Driven by a passion for wildlife, they believe that ecotourism is the best option to benefit their communities.

« Joseph Masibo

Although born and brought up near the Kakamega Forest in Kenya's Western Province, Joseph's spiritual home is the Masai Mara. For it is here, amongst the abundant wildlife of the savannahs that he has spent almost every day of his 15-year career doing what he is most passionate about – guiding his guests. While he began his working life as a field co-ordinator for an aid agency, his heart was always set on a life in the bush. An opportunity arose in 1990, and with encouragement and guidance from his mentor, Jonathan Scott, the well-known Kenyan wildlife photographer and television presenter, Joseph rapidly established himself as a respected guide. He is now Head Ranger over 19 rangers based at CC Africa's Bateleur Camp and Kichwa Tembo Tented Camp. Articulate, thoroughly professional, and blessed with the most charming of demeanors, Joseph is also part of the camps' senior management team and works as a facilitator and tutor on the company's community conservation projects through the Africa Foundation.

Food for thought

East Africa is a culinary delight. Its history of settlement has created a cuisine that blends the spicy and aromatic foods of the Arab and Oriental world with traditional European and local fare. Whether on safari or eating out in a city or resort restaurant, your taste buds will be well catered for.

Abdi Haruna, the head chef at Greystoke Mahale in the Mahale Mountains National Park, Tanzania, presents his favourite fish dishes prepared from fresh kuhe (one of the larger cichlid species) and mussels taken from the waters of Lake Tanganyika.

Kuhe Shushimi – Served as a pre-dinner bar snack within hours of being caught. Fillet the fish and remove the skin before finely slicing into thin strips. Serve with a soy sauce mixed with grated ginger and a touch of freshly squeezed lime juice as a dip, and wasabi on the side.

Lake Mussels – Served as a starter. Clean and gently remove mussels from the shell before boiling for a few minutes. Fry chopped onion, garlic and wild mushrooms separately before adding as a topping. Replace into the shell before serving.

Kuhe – The larger fish are served as the main course, cut into fillets before they are lightly fried in Italian olive oil. Steamed baby carrots and baby corn are served as the vegetables of choice. Add a filling of fried wild mushrooms between sections of fillets and present the fish serving on a banana leaf. No sauces added.

Fresh Tropical Fruits – Served as a dessert. A selection of mango, watermelon, papaya and pineapple, presented on a freshly cut banana leaf.

Greystoke Ginger Beer – Grate wild ginger and mix into a paste with freshly squeezed lemon juice and brown sugar. To drink, add chilled soda water or still bottled water.

George Musembi, head chef at Bateleur Camp in the Masai Mara, Kenya, usually prepares traditional Kenyan food for Friday dinner. It is customary for most Kenyan households to get together on this day for a large family meal.

Avocado and tomato – Served as a starter. Take a half avocado, peel and serve with sliced tomato on the side. Add freshly squeezed lemon juice to taste.

Fresh Mombasa Prawns – Served as a main course. Peel and wash the prawns before marinating them in fresh lemon juice, garlic and olive oil for an hour. The prawns are put onto a skewer and then lightly grilled on a charcoal grill. George affirms that the smoke from the grill adds to the flavouring. The side sauce of garlic, butter and lemon juice, as typically served all over the world, is prepared along with a traditional chutney sauce known as *kachumbari*. This spicy condiment consists of chopped onion and chopped seedless tomatoes mixed with salt, coriander and hot peppers.

Irio – A mashed vegetable mix served with the prawns. A selection of freshly picked beans, potatoes and sweet corn are boiled separately before they are mashed together and sprinkled with coriander.

Sukumawiki – Kenyan spinach served as a second vegetable dish with the prawns. Freshly picked leaves are sautéed with garlic and chopped onions before a dollop of cream is stirred in. This Swahili word, literally translated, means 'to push the week'. It is often eaten as a main dish in many poorer Kenyan households when there is insufficient money for meat, fish or maize porridge. The name is a reference to stretching the budget until the next week's wages are received.

Ndizi Choma – Grilled banana served as a dessert. Grill ripe bananas in their skins before peeling. A topping of caramelised macadamia nuts is then poured over the bananas.

Bateleur Dawa – The word *dawa* means medicine in Swahili, but don't be put off as this tasty local cocktail makes for a great pre- or after-dinner drink. A double shot of vodka, two teaspoons of honey and freshly squeezed lime juice are stirred and served in a tumbler with plenty of crushed ice.

Opposite top: The migration reaches the northern Serengeti and Masai Mara in August and starts heading south again in November.
Opposite bottom: Cruising the forested shoreline of Lake Tanganyika.
Above: Micro-lighting over Lake Manyara.
Left: Greystoke Mahale, one of East Africa's finest lodges, is on the shores of Lake Tanganyika.

Pages 124–125:
*Tanzania has no more
than 1 500
chimpanzees left in
the wild.*
Pages 126–127: *Lake
Nakuru National Park
offers the most
rewarding rhino
viewing in Kenya.*
This spread:
*The 'great migration',
with almost 1.5 million
wildebeest making up
the vast majority of
animals, is the most
impressive large-
mammal phenomenon
on the planet.*

Page 130, top: *During the driest months of August to November, hippo gather in the remaining pools of the Katuma River, Katavi National Park.*

Page 130, bottom: *Once the rivers have dried out, the crocodiles in the Katuma River gather at the few remaining damp spots.*

Page 131, top: *The wildebeest of East Africa are a sub-species known as the white-bearded wildebeest.*

Page 131, bottom: *Leopard, while not seen so often, occur in larger numbers than lion and cheetah.*

Right: *Although habitat destruction is taking its toll, Sykes monkeys are widely distributed along the Kenyan coast. They are omnivorous, arboreal and territorial, with the troop size averaging 20 individuals.*

De Fassa's waterbuck amongst a grove of fever acacias in Nakuru National Park.

Opposite, top: *Grevy's Zebra, an endangered species, is found in the drier northern region of Kenya.*
Opposite, bottom: *A white-backed vulture sees off a black-backed jackal at a kill site in the Masai Mara.*
Left: *A lappet-faced vulture caught in the late afternoon glow of a Masai Mara thunderstorm.*
Page 136: *The kori bustard, Africa's heaviest flying bird, is commonly seen in the drier regions of Kenya.*
Page 137: *White storks are common summer migrants to the savannahs of East Africa.*

East Africa's fauna and flora enjoy a unique position in Africa. The region straddles several African biomes: southern African woodland, West African tropical forest and East African savannah. Add the Great Rift Valley and its associated volcanoes, lakes and highland regions, almost 2 000 kilometres of coastline and various marine environments, and the result is an astonishingly rich diversity of animal and plant life.

Under threat

Despite the efforts of various wildlife authorities tasked with managing the biodiversity, a number of wilderness areas and species in both countries face major threats. In some instances, these threats require urgent attention at local, regional and national levels. Kenya's position is more urgent, as a large percentage of the wildlife is found outside nationally protected areas. In Tanzania, the majority of wildlife populations are found within national parks and reserves.

As is the case throughout the continent, the threats come primarily from increasing human pressures and the unsustainable use and harvesting of natural resources. Illegal commercial activities such as poaching, trawling and logging are also having a major impact, and poor and ineffective management has exacerbated the situation. Here are some of the concerns:

• Over the last 25 years, Kenya has lost over 50% of its large mammal populations.

All Kenya's forest habitats are under threat from charcoal-cutters, commercial logging and 'slash and burn' clearing for human settlement and agriculture. Many of the group ranches that occur on the edges of Kenya's national parks have an over-population of domestic stock, placing unsustainable pressures on the habitat.

• Habitat destruction in western Tanzania threatens the chimpanzee populations in Gombe Stream National Park, and, to a lesser extent, in the Mahale Mountains. There are no more than 1 500 chimps left in the wild.

• East Africa has a number of important bird areas, many lying outside protected areas. They are under threat. BirdLife International lists 36 species in Tanzania and 27 in Kenya as threatened. Three of these – the taita thrush and taita apalis in south-east Kenya, and the long-billed tailorbird in the eastern Usumbaras in northern Tanzania – are on the critical list, with a high risk of extinction.

• All the lakes in East Africa are under threat, with some critically endangered. Lake Victoria, for example, is losing its cichlid diversity and over 200 species have been lost in the last 25 years. The two causes have been predation by Nile Perch, which were foolishly introduced by man in the late 1950s, and eutrophication, which is a form of pollution also occurring in certain other lakes. Excessive nutrient buildup in the water – caused by deforestation, urban sewage, and nitrogen and phosphorus accumulation from farming practices – promotes excessive algal bloom, which in turn makes for turbid and warmer water. Lake Naivasha in Kenya suffers from intense human pressures around its shores, including chemical pollution from the cut-flower industry.

• Commercial and subsistence poaching are a major threat to the plains game species in a number of parks and reserves in both countries. Particularly badly affected in Kenya are Tsavo East, Tsavo West and all the northern parks. In Tanzania, the same goes for the western boundary of the Serengeti and the game reserves in the central regions.

• In Tanzania, there is a need to afford protection to crucial wildlife migratory corridors and seasonal grazing areas that lie outside certain parks and reserves. The dry-season regions around Lakes Manyara and Tarangire, and the corridors linking Kigosi Game Reserve, Ugalla River Game Reserve and Ruaha National Park are examples. Lake Natron in northern Tanzania is the largest and most important breeding site for lesser flamingos; over 3 million birds breed here annually, yet it is not a protected area.

• Marine environments are in decline. The Kenyan coastline and Zanzibar Island in particular suffer from high-volume tourism, urban pollution and uncontrolled and illegal fishing activities.

Opposite: *Because of increasing human pressures, unsustainable levels of natural resource exploitation is occurring in many regions of East Africa.*

Science and conservation

We have provided a list, by no means complete, of private and quasi-government bodies involved in research and conservation work. Their efforts are crucial to the future security and wellbeing of the region's biodiversity. Many of these organisations rely on private funding and donations to carry out this work, and they also take on volunteer workers for varying periods. Anyone wishing to get involved, either as a volunteer or with financial aid, may contact them at the addresses given.

TANZANIA

Wildlife Conservation Society of Tanzania (WCST) – Tanzania's only national conservation body promotes various ecological initiatives and educational programmes from branches in Arusha and Dar es Salaam. Tel: +255 22 2112518, e-mail: wcst@africaonline.co.tz, website: www.wcstarusha.org

Tanzania Wildlife Research Institute (TAWIRI) – Coordinates and monitors wildlife research projects in Tanzania. Tel: +255 27 2507796, e-mail: enquiries@tawiri.org, website: www.tawiri.org

African Conservation Foundation – International body that works to preserve Africa's wild heritage. Website: www.africanconservation.org

BirdLife International – Worldwide body that promotes conservation of birds and their ecosystems. Website: www.birdlife.net

The Jane Goodall Institute – Founded by Jane Goodall, the well-known primate researcher. The Institute has since become a global body involved in general research, education and conservation. Website: www.janegoodall.org

African Wildlife Foundation – This global body has a regional office in Arusha from where they operate a number of scientific research and community-based conservation initiatives throughout the country. Tel: +255 27 2909616, website: www.awf.org

The George Adamson Wildlife Preservation Trust – This trust is primarily involved in the development and management of the Mkomazi Game Reserve in northern Tanzania. Tel: +255 27 2752793, e-mail: info@mkomazi.com, website: www.georgeadamson.org

GTZ – This German development agency is involved in community-based conservation projects. Tel: +255 22 2866065, e-mail: scp@africaonline.co.tz, website: www.wildlife-programme.gtz.de

KENYA

The David Sheldrick Wildlife Trust – While the focus species are elephant and rhino, this Nairobi National Park-based trust is involved in a variety of conservation measures from anti-poaching to relocation in Tsavo National Park. Tel: +254 20 891996, e-mail: rc-h@africaonline.co.ke, website: www.sheldrickwildlifetrust.org

Lewa Wildlife Conservancy – A private group involved in the conservation of wildlife and habitats in the Laikipia district. Tel: +254 20 607893, e-mail: info@lewa.org, website: www.lewa.org

BirdLife International – Worldwide body that promotes conservation of birds and their ecosystems. Website: www.birdlife.net

Laikipia Wildlife Forum – A local group that works with a number of stakeholders from the Laikipia district to conserve the region's ecosystems for the benefit of all. Tel: +254 62 31600, e-mail: lwf@africaonline.co.ke, website: www.laikipia.org

East African Wildlife Society – The society is involved in wildlife conservation and fundraising, primarily in Kenya. Tel: +254 20 3874145, website: www.eawildlife.org

Local Ocean Trust – Based in Watamu and involved with the conservation and educational aspects of protecting Kenya's marine environment. Turtles are the focus species. Tel: +254 42 32118, e-mail: wtwkenya@swiftmalindi.com

The Colobus Trust – Based in Diani Beach and involved with protecting the limited natural coastal habitat that remains for a number of primate species occurring south of Mombasa. Tel: +254 40 3203519, e-mail: info@colobustrust.org, website: www.colobustrust.org

DR PETER MORKEL

He does not keep a tally, but it is well known that Dr Peter Morkel has relocated nearly 1 000 black rhinoceros and more than 400 white rhinoceros in more than 25 years of work as a veterinary scientist and conservationist. It is no wonder then that he is regarded by his peers, both locally and internationally, as Africa's leading rhino relocation expert. This work has covered southern, Central and East Africa, and has earned him the distinction of being the only vet to have seen every sub-species of black and white rhino.

Although southern Africa is his home – he was born in Zimbabwe, studied at Onderstepoort in South Africa and worked as a vet and game capture specialist mainly in South Africa, Namibia and Botswana – he is now based in the Ngorongoro Crater in Tanzania where he is the Rhino Co-ordinator for the Frankfurt Zoological Society. They provide the financial support that enables Peter, who works in partnership with the management of the Ngorongoro Conservation Area, to carry out his crucial work of ensuring the survival of the region's endangered black rhino population. Heavy poaching in the 1970s and 1980s reduced the crater population from over 100 animals to fewer than five, before conservation efforts stabilised the situation. Today there are 19, and the crater remains the best place to view black rhino in Tanzania.

Peter's work not only includes monitoring and the security of the rhino, but also involvement in managing the ecology of the greater Ngorongoro region, as 'the management of the overall ecology will be crucial to the success of this population'.

ISLAND STYLE

Travelling East Africa has countless joys, of which none is greater than the opportunity to combine a wildlife safari with a tropical island getaway. Tanzania is spoilt for choice, with the **Zanzibar Archipelago** and **Mafia Island**, while Kenya has the **Lamu Archipelago** and a scattering of islets in the far south, all of them within easy reach of the continental mainland. They offer fantastic diving and snorkelling, palm-lined beaches and soothing waters for washing away the safari dust, and an **enviable choice of lodgings**, some of which come with all the tropical trimmings you might expect of an island paradise.

Factfile

• East Africa's coastal climate is influenced by two alternating and distinctive seasons, the south-east monsoons (*kuzi* to the locals), which blow from May to October, and the north-east monsoons (*kaskazi*), which blow from November to March.

• These wind patterns are the most important climatic features affecting the ocean currents, water temperatures and human activity.

Cyclones do occur to the south of the region, but the East African coastline is seldom affected.

• The dominant current is the East African Coastal Current, which flows from south to north along the continental mainland.

• The region's waters are tropical, with average daily temperatures ranging between 20 °C and 30 °C.

• Pemba Island is a granite outcrop that probably broke away from the mainland approximately 10 million years ago. Zanzibar and Mafia Islands are composed mostly of fossilised coral rock and were once part of an extensive reef system linked to the mainland. They became separated less than 5 million years ago with rising waters and erosion. The sandy islands of the Lamu Archipelago were once part of the continental mainland.

Previous spread: *A cargo dhow approaches Lamu Town in the Lamu Archipelago.*
Left: *The dining room view from Chumbe Island Coral Park off Zanzibar Island.*

The Zanzibar Archipelago

Zanzibar is a place of many **alluring images**. The name alone conjures mystery and the aroma of spices, exotic architecture and the majestic sailing ships of these waters, the dhows. The island is rich in the history of the mariners who established Zanzibar as the strategic and commercial centre of the **Swahili Coast.** They came from the Middle East and the Orient as traders and slavers, as sultans and kings, and were followed in later centuries by the European adventurers, explorers and missionaries. Together, they forged the legendary Swahili civilisation and its rich culture, and embarked upon a period of peace and prosperity.

The single factor that cemented Zanzibar's position as the centre of commercial and political power in East Africa was the slave trade. This practice, that still today ranks as one of the worst crimes perpetrated against humanity, reached its peak during the 19th century, when over 50 000 Africans a year were being captured for sale to colonial masters. Trading caravans would head into the interior regions of mainland Africa to acquire slaves and ivory in exchange for weapons, food supplies, cloth, porcelain, glass and money. During the reign of the Omani Arabs, the trading caravans established Zanzibar as the major port of export for both slaves and ivory.

The central market for **trading in slaves** was in Stone Town, in what is now the Anglican Cathedral courtyard. Before the slaves were auctioned off, they were bound to a whipping post and subjected to a lashing, in order to determine their physical strength and endurance of pain. The most stoical slaves fetched the highest prices. Once sold, most were shipped off for a life of hard labour in foreign lands, though some stayed behind to work the spice and coconut plantations on Zanzibar and Pemba. Some estimates suggest that over 600 000 slaves were sold during the 19th century.

The beginning of the end of the slave trade in Zanzibar was the Moresby Treaty of 1822, which banned the sale of slaves to Christian powers. Although the slave markets were closed down in 1873, slavery only finally disappeared from Zanzibar in the mid 1890s.

Present-day Zanzibar is characterised by the verve and charm of its now less-prosperous population, and offers languid days spent sun-soaking on palm-lined beaches, occasionally taking to the azure tropical waters to dive and snorkel at leisure. The archipelago is an **enticing destination** with untold options, most of which are extremely affordable.

If you wish to visit a number of coastal hotels and lodges, and the interior as well as Stone Town, there are in essence two ways to plan your trip. The conventional way is to pre-book your destinations and day trips, complete with all transfers, before arrival. This is hassle-free, and you can travel in air-conditioned mini-buses. Unfortunately, you miss much of the cultural experience when you only see the roadside along the shortest routes between destinations. A far more rewarding option, particularly for those with time to spare, is to arrive with only your first Stone Town stop pre-booked, spend a few days absorbing the ways of the island, then hire your own 4x4 or small motorbike and simply head out. Pemba Island to the north is best reached by taking a charter flight from Stone Town.

STONE TOWN HIGHLIGHTS

The Stone Town ramble – Stone Town is one of Africa's historical wonders, and amongst the walls, minarets and spires lies the incredible legacy of East Africa's fabled era of commercial and cultural pre-eminence. With almost 2 000 ancient stone buildings reflecting the fusion of its Arabic, Persian, Indian and European heritage, the town is an architectural delight. Take to the network of narrow and bustling alleyways and discover neighbourhoods no guidebook has ever mentioned.

A night at Emerson and Green – No matter what budget constraints you have, stretch them and live like a sultan for a night or two in the pick of Stone Town's hotels. It's the ultimate the island has to offer in Zanzibar style. Bedrooms, bathrooms, balconies, passageways and restaurants, all have been restored with exquisite authenticity. Time spent in this hotel is a trip back into the history and lifestyle of a more prosperous past.

Sundowners and dinner at Mercury's – Arrive before sunset, grab a seafront table, and spend the next few hours soaking up the Stone Town vibe. Cocktails are always on order, and after having toasted the setting sun, tuck into a menu offering a seafood fiesta. With stunning views and an island-style ambience, Mercury's is the choice one-stop restaurant and bar for locals and tourists alike.

Fumba day trip – A great day trip south of Stone Town from the village of Fumba. Safari Blue has a number of dhows that take you into the Menai Bay conservation area, with an excellent chance at close-up encounters with dolphins. Break for some snorkelling and a sumptuous seafood lunch on an island before racing for home under full sail in the late afternoon winds.

Festival of the Dhow Countries – If it's carnival time you're after, travel at the end of June and into July when this annual festival is held by the historical Indian Ocean trading nations. The whole of Zanzibar comes alive as the cultures of the region merge to showcase their film, music, dance, art and theatre in a week of festivities. The focus of the festival is in Stone Town, but the whole of Zanzibar celebrates as travelling acts move across the island taking the arts to the people.

COASTAL HIGHLIGHTS

Chumbe Island Coral Park – This rustic island hideaway is a must, and you should plan to stay a night or two. With its spectacular coral garden and pristine forest reserve, Chumbe is the pride of Zanzibar's natural heritage, complementing the vast savannah ecosystems of mainland Tanzania. Chumbe was developed as a fully sustainable eco-tourism-based conservation project. Everything about this magical and private island leaves one feeling inspired about the natural world and how we should be co-operating with it.

Mnemba Island Lodge – This stunning, recently renovated lodge exudes a sense of exclusivity and style. It lies on a tiny island just off the north-east coast on the spectacular diving reefs of the Mnemba Atoll, with pristine beaches sweeping its entire shoreline. The lodge is tucked in amidst a forest. Whether your dream is to experience the ultimate honeymoon paradise, dive the days away, or merely relax, Mnemba makes it come true.

Below left: *The main dhow harbour in Stone Town.* **Below right:** *Stone Town is the most authentic example of a Swahili trading town, and is characterised by its maze of narrow alleyways.*

Matemwe Bungalows – Situated opposite Mnemba Atoll on the north-east coast guarding a promontory of fossilised coral rock, Matemwe is one of the more secluded beach destinations. It's stylish yet simple, with no designer clutter, just those honest homely comforts and qualities that make you want to stay and stay.

Shooting Star Lodge – Perched up high on a coral rock outcrop, this rustic lodging is possibly Zanzibar's best-kept secret. The spectacular sea views alone are worth the very affordable daily rate. Elly Mlang'a is the most engaging of hosts, and with the laid-back and intimate atmosphere, you have a gem of a getaway.

Ras Nungwi Beach Hotel – The pick of Zanzibar's larger beach lodges and hotels, and your best bet on the northern Nungwi tip. The hotel's size is most definitely offset by the charm and comforts of the surroundings. Divers have access to the superb coral reefs of the Mnemba Atoll, and for the land-lubbers, the beaches stretch forever.

Breezes Beach Club and **The Palms** – These two sister lodges lying side-by-side are the choice destinations on the south-east coast. Breezes is the larger of the two, and offers all the style, comfort and facilities you can expect of a premier tropical island resort, while The Palms, complete with a full spa, offers a more private and elegant option with the most extravagant and luxurious bedrooms on the island.

PEMBA ISLAND

Separated from Zanzibar Island by the swirling waters of the 60-kilometre-wide Zanzibar Channel, the archipelago's most northerly island is a mere forty minutes or so in a light charter aircraft from Stone Town, or half a day's dhow ride from Zanzibar's northern tip. Although less developed and less visited than its southern neighbour, Pemba is as worthwhile a destination, and for the more adventurous traveller in search of remoteness, it is in many ways a superior choice.

Fundu Lagoon, set amidst a dense and pristine coastal forest on a low hilltop along the Wambaa Peninsula on the island's western side, is the prize destination. There's a gratifying remoteness here that you are unlikely to experience elsewhere on the archipelago. The extremely comfortable lodge, with a wonderful sundowner deck out front, offers a full range of water-sport activities, including some of the archipelago's best dive sites, and cultural visits to the nearby villages.

Below left: *Spices and grains on display in the Darajani Market, Stone Town.* **Below right:** *Outrigger dhows, known locally as ngalawas, are the fishing vessels of choice.* **Next spread:** *A fly fisherman's haul from Manda Bay. What is not required for the table gets released back into the water.*

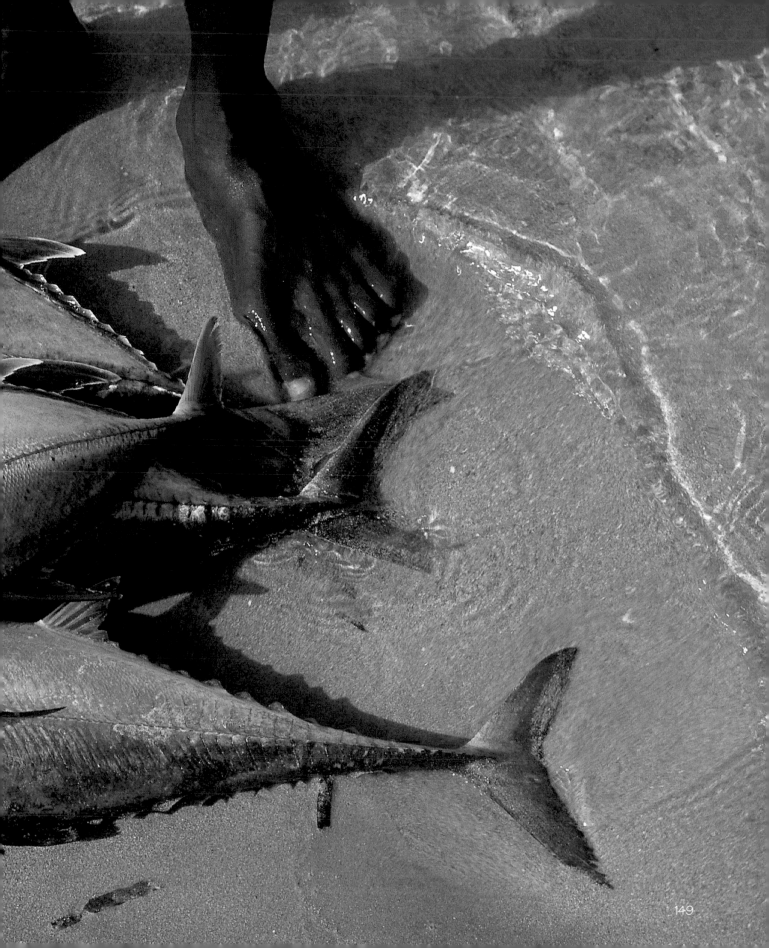

The Lamu Archipelago

The name Lamu is given to a district in the Coastal Province of Kenya, but also to the archipelago, to one of its islands, and to the largest town on the island. The word is thought to be a popularised derivative of Amu, the name used by locals for the town. Comprising four large islands, **Lamu**, **Manda**, **Paté** and **Kiwaihu**, and a number of smaller islets, the archipelago lies in an extended inlet along Kenya's far northern coast, and a short distance south of the border with Somalia. The islands are mostly uninhabited because of a lack of fresh water. They are interlinked by densely-vegetated mangrove channels, some of which are not navigable at low tide. The region is populated mostly by Bajunis (coastal Bantu people), Somalis, Orma, and those of Arab and Indian descent who are involved in fishing, tourism and the sale of mangrove poles.

Over a period of almost four centuries, the region was the base for a number of powerful sultanate city-states that became the northernmost frontier of Swahili culture. Remnants of this legacy are still visible today when visiting the town of Lamu. UNESCO declared Lamu a World Heritage Site in 2001, describing it as '**the oldest and best-preserved Swahili settlement in East Africa**'.

Although Arab traders first established settlements on the islands as early as the 9th century, it was not until the 14th century that the region began its rise to prominence under the sultanate of Paté. Controlled by an Omani clan involved in trading ivory, mangrove poles and slaves, the island-state's supremacy lasted well into the late 1700s despite numerous battles with the Portuguese. It was during the early 1800s that the power base shifted to Lamu, when Oman declared it a protectorate in 1813, and the island's forces defeated those of Paté in a battle on the beaches of nearby Shela. It was the height of the ivory and the slave trade, and with the Sultans of Zanzibar using the naturally protected channel as a slave transit and trading post, Lamu soon established itself as one of the coastline's wealthiest and most impressive towns. The town's fortunes began to slide after the British enforced the abolition of the slave trade in Zanzibar, and by the end of the 1800s the boom was over. Lamu became a British Protectorate in 1890 and was incorporated into Kenya at independence in 1963.

LAMU ISLAND

While all the islands have tourist facilities, Lamu's historical significance has made it by far the most popular. Adding to the appeal is its celebrated status amongst some of the world's **aristocracy and Bohemian set** as

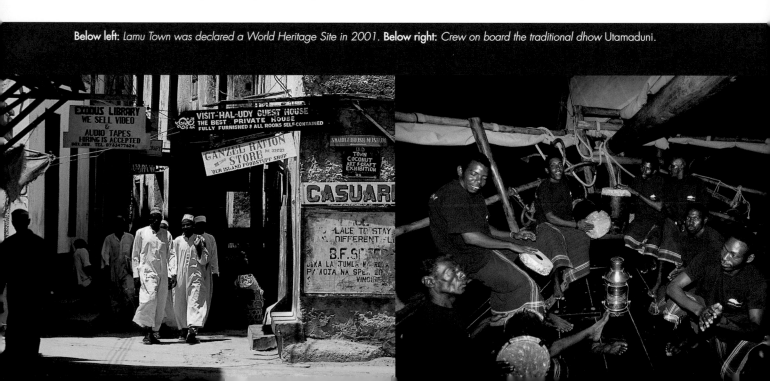

Below left: *Lamu Town was declared a World Heritage Site in 2001.* **Below right:** *Crew on board the traditional dhow Utamaduni.*

a favoured hangout. Since the 1970s, they have been drawn by its geographical obscurity, natural charm and cultural character. Today many of the homes in the village of **Shela** are owned by famous and wealthy foreigners.

A preferable alternative to the glitz and glamour of Shela is **Lamu Town**, a 30-minute walk away along the waterfront. It still retains much of its original Swahili character, and in the words of a local writer on Lamu's history, '**has been spared the disruption of its society by Western influences**'. Spend time here mingling with the locals and absorbing their customary way of life. They are most welcoming, and the best way to make their acquaintance is by strolling the bustling waterfront, or exploring the maze of narrow alleyways snaking their way through the town. Finding good food can be problematic, but the town does serve the most heavenly fresh fruit juices, and in the evenings, your best bet is to follow the locals to find the best Swahili fare. If you need land transport, it's best to make do with a donkey or a bicycle, as vehicular traffic here is rather impractical. Dhow rides, museum and castle tours, and beach excursions are all on offer (Lamu World in front of Salama House is the best choice), as are fishing and snorkelling trips to the deeper waters beyond.

Salama House and **Azania House**, two adjoining Swahili homes magnificently restored and adapted to modern use, are the prime places to stay. They are centrally situated, have an indoor swimming pool, and serve superb food, and the third-floor balconies have inviting town and sea views.

MANDA ISLAND

For sheer charm, fun and privacy, **Manda Bay** on Manda Island is certainly the pick of the archipelago, and a candidate for East Africa's essential great escape. Its superb location, set amongst whispering coconut palms on the very tip of the island, offers sweeping ocean vistas, and a prime position for both sunrises and sunsets. Like any true beach haven, the ambiance is **seductively island-style**, laid-back and carefree, yet extremely comfortable and stylish. There are loads of boating possibilities, including a magnificent 60-foot traditional dhow, bill-fishing rigs and ski-boats, so the active set are well catered for. Lamu Island is a mere 20-minute boat-ride away, and on the small island just offshore lie the Manda Ruins, an ancient Swahili archaeological site dating back to the 9th century. Manda is also great for just chilling, with plenty of comfy cushions, chairs to lounge about in and, of course, the beach.

Below left: *Donkeys and bicycles are the only form of transport in Lamu Town.* **Below right:** *Manda Bay is a candidate for the title of East Africa's prime beach destination.*

Above: *Lamu Town is one of the best preserved Swahili towns along the East Africa coastline.*
Opposite: *Swahili boy from Lamu Town.*

Mafia Island

With a name like this, maybe it isn't too surprising that Mafia is the least-known of all the region's island destinations. It is often incorrectly believed to be part of the Zanzibar Archipelago, but in fact it belongs to mainland Tanzania. Lying a mere 120 kilometres south of Dar es Salaam and an even shorter distance off the delta of the Rufiji River, Mafia is the only reasonably sized island (394 square kilometres) of a small archipelago containing seven other smaller islands and a number of tiny outcrops. The name has nothing to do with the notorious Italian 'mob', but is thought to be derived either from the Arabic word *morfieyeh*, meaning 'a group', or from the name of a tribe of Arabic people, the Ma'afir, who once ruled the islands.

The archipelago has a **colourful history** going back over 2 000 years, which is when the first settlers, Bantu people from the mainland, are thought to have arrived. Once the Arabic traders began arriving, and a Shirazi dynasty established the first permanent settlement in 975 AD, Mafia became an important trading post, reaching its zenith between the 12th and 15th centuries. Periods of conquest and occupation by European, Arabic and Malagasy powers followed – the Portuguese in the 1500s, various Omani Sultans during the 1600s and 1700s, Sakalava cannibals from Madagascar in the early 1800s, the Germans in the late 1800s and the British for a short period in the early 1900s. Finally the islands were incorporated into Tanganyika in 1922. Mafia has been something of a tranquil backwater since then.

Although **characteristically tropical**, Mafia does not have the tourism infrastructure of its northern neighbours. It is best suited for divers, snorkellers and fishermen, and those seeking a remote experience without the cultural and commercial distractions of Zanzibar. Chole Mjini on Chole Island, and Kinasi Lodge and Pole Pole Resort on Mafia Island are all great accommodation options offering the full range of water sports. Look out, though, for new developments in upcoming years, as a number of mainland operators have their sights firmly set on Mafia.

Below: *Snorkelling off Manda Bay.*
Opposite: *A bedroom view from the recently restored Salama House in Lamu Town.*
Next spread: *Manda Bay has its own 60-foot traditional dhow for sunset, day or overnight trips.*

OUT OF THE WAY

There is always a sense of comfort in sticking to the recognised routes, but they often lack the challenges and rewards that come with tackling 'out of the way' options or 'undiscovered' places. Some of these are truly far-flung, requiring days of arduous travel, but others are right on the doorstep, and get overlooked for no apparent reason.

Both Tanzania and Kenya are large countries, and the outlying regions, free of the foreign cultural contamination so commonly encountered along the beaten tracks of Africa, and devoid of thronging tourists, offer more than a simple holiday destination. For the **adventurous of spirit,** these are compelling reasons to head out and beyond, but caution is advised: double-check with the locals on conditions, and make sure you are self-sufficient, particularly with regard to fuel and water, as local villages may have only rudimentary supplies.

Previous spread: *Overlooking Lake Natron, one of Tanzania's largest soda lakes.*
Below: *Lake Eyasi with the Eyasi escarpment in the distance.*

Tanzania

LAKE EYASI

Although it lies close to Tanzania's busy Northern Circuit, Lake Eyasi somehow still escapes the attention of many visitors. It's just over two hours by road from the Ngorongoro Crater, or four hours from Arusha, the last 45 kilometres being on a fairly poor dirt road, before the rather drab landscapes unravel to reveal the delightful oasis formed by the shores of one of the Rift Valley's oldest lakes. Saline and seasonal, the 75-kilometre-long lake is hemmed in by the Eyasi Escarpment running along the northern shoreline, the Kidero Mountains to the south, and the region's highest point, Mount Oldeani (3 185 metres), looming over the lake's eastern edges. Once past the village of Man'gola, head straight for **Kisema Ngeda, a delightfully rustic and comfortable tented camp** nestled in amongst an impressive grove of palm tress on the eastern shoreline.

Lake Eyasi's attractions lie not only in the stark splendour of its surroundings, but also in its unique cultural experiences. The region is home to the Hadzabe people who, along with the Sandawe from the central regions, are thought to be Tanzania's earliest inhabitants. Perhaps as long as 10 000 years ago, these hunter-gatherers settled the dry lands of Eyasi and its greater environs to pursue their semi-nomadic lifestyle. Like the Khoisan people of southern Africa, they speak a language characterised by clicks, and live in small family groups. Despite their historical presence and claims to the land, they too are facing a tragic situation of marginalisation and alienation. Land pressures from other groups, the Barabaig, Iraqw and Maasai predominately, are dispossessing the Hadzabe of their traditional lands, while the government fails to offer them any form of protection. Witnessing such a plight is never pleasant, but spending time with these **fascinating and incredibly humble people** may just help them towards securing a future.

With a mix of scrub, dry woodland and the wetlands surrounding the lake, the region also offers birders a **surprisingly interesting species list**. Lake Eyasi is most definitely worth a few days at least.

LAKE NATRON AND OL DONYO LENGAI

Like Lake Eyasi, Lake Natron and the volcano Ol Donyo Lengai (2 878 metres) lie within the backyard of the main attractions in the north. Yet despite this proximity, comparatively few people venture this way, giving these dry lands a sense of remoteness. **Lake Natron** is Tanzania's largest soda lake, stretching for 60 kilometres, and with the rugged rift valley ranges lining the western and eastern shores, the setting is one of stark and barren beauty.

Ol Donyo Lengai, guarding Natron's southern extremity, is Tanzania's only active volcano, and a sacred mountain to the Maasai people. The Maasai name means 'the Mountain of God', and since numerous eruptions have occurred over the last few centuries, the power and mystique associated with their god Enkai are well established. Besides the awesome scenery, being here also offers opportunities for **mixing with the Maasai** and absorbing the ways of their fascinating culture, and for the fitter folk, a chance of a full day's climb into the volcano.

Access is from the main Arusha-Nairobi road, or from the Serengeti National Park to the west. There is a small community-run campsite with basic bandas (chalets) on the shores of the lake.

TANZANIA'S SOUTH-EAST

This route covers the vast and somewhat isolated south-eastern regions of Tanzania that are home to the Makonde people. Starting either at Mbeya or Dar es Salaam, it could be extended into a lengthy circular journey that takes in the coastline road that runs up from Mtwara and past the **ancient Swahili ruins** of **Kilwa Kisiwani** and **Songo Mnara**. About 350 kilometres south of Dar, these ruins, lying on two small islands just off the mainland, bear testimony to the more prosperous times of the region and are regarded as some of the most outstanding examples of the coral masonry so characteristic of the Swahili people.

At present, the whole region remains relatively undeveloped, but aid agencies are beginning to move in with funding for infrastructural work, so that in a few years' time travelling here will be a lot less

Above left: *Every day is market day in Lushoto, Usumbara Mountains.* **Above right:** *The mountain pass road leading up to Lushoto.*

challenging. Meanwhile in the far south, for example, once you have left Songea, the roads become tricky, particularly in the wet season when they may be impassable. The same can be said for the road coming from Dar once you have crossed the Rufiji River. It is definitely advisable to **check road conditions** before tackling these parts of the country. This circuit will include every element of what makes Tanzania such a compelling destination.

USUMBARA MOUNTAINS

Inexplicably, these mountains are a seldom-mentioned destination, yet they make for a charming and extremely affordable diversion from the wildlife safari circuit. The turn-off is at the small town of Mombo on the main Dar-Arusha road, and within a few kilometres, the road begins winding its way up into the yonder. The mountains, a part of the greater Eastern Arc chain, are split into a western and eastern range, and although they are densely populated in some areas, there is that **sense of rural tranquility** that one finds in mountainous environments. The deforestation is distressing, but there is still enough greenery for the flora fundis to get stuck into the range's **immense plant diversity**. Head for **Muller's Mountain Lodge** beyond Lushoto, the regional centre, and enter a world of hiking, birding and mountain-biking in forested peaks. The less agile may just settle for utter relaxation.

Kenya

LAKE TURKANA

These searing northern semi-desert regions, known as the Northern Frontier District during colonial times, are the most remote and **some of the most unique and exciting areas** to travel in Kenya. Because of past problems with Somali bandits, they still get referred to as the 'badlands'. While this tag should not put you off, it's always best to do some homework with local operators before heading this way. First choice would be to join a mobile tented operator, but if you are doing your own thing, then stick to the main routes. Even these don't see much traffic. You can't go wrong by heading up the dirt road that winds through the inspiring Mathews Range north of Samburu National Park and past Maralal, a small dusty frontier town. From here it's a long haul to the lava flows on the southern shores of Lake Turkana, the village of Loyangalani and beyond.

Although Turkana's water levels fluctuate widely, it covers approximately 6 400 square kilometres, making it the **largest desert lake in the world** and the dominant feature of these northern landscapes. Geologists believe it to have been even larger in the past; the geology of the region indicates a massive body of water that may have extended south towards Lake Baringo, and possibly connected to the Nile system.

The first European explorer to be awed by its impressive size and raw beauty was Count Samuel Teleki von Szek, who gave it the colonial era name of Lake Rudolf after his friend, Crown Prince Rudolf of Austria. For others, the more poetic name 'Jade Sea' has greater appeal. The lake lies in a hot and arid region and is fed principally by the Omo River flowing from the Ethiopian Highlands to the north. Turkana has no outlet for its waters and extremely high evaporation levels occur. The resulting **mineral salt buildup gives the waters their sparkling jade colour**.

Within the lake are a number of volcanic islands, two of which, South Island and Central Island, are national parks and have become famous for the number and size of their **Nile crocodiles**. Opposite Central Island on the eastern shore lies Sibiloi National Park, better known for the archaeological discoveries made here by the Leakey family than for its wildlife. An alternative return route heads east and then south through Marsabit National Park and back to Samburu and the town of Isiolo.

GARSEN AND GARISSA

The arid and flat hinterlands of Kenya's northern coast around Garsen, extending inland to Garissa, offer a fascinating glimpse into the life of **various ethnic groups**. The roads can be a little harsh, but time spent amongst the Orma, Somali and Rendille people makes up for all the corrugations and sandy stretches you are likely to encounter.

THE ABERDARES

Tucked away within the central regions between Nairobi and Nanyuki, the Aberdares are an often-overlooked mountainous hideaway. Head for one of the Kenya Wildlife Service campsites or book a few nights in one of the banda units and spend time exploring the **lush montane forests** and upland moors. Elephant, buffalo and a variety of antelope species are common sightings, and for fly-fishermen, there are a number of sparkling streams within the upper reaches.

Left: *Camels are kept by most of the ethnic groups living in Northern Kenya.*
Page 164: *Roadside enticements in the Usumbara Mountains.*
Page 165: *A Somali woman leads her camels, strapped with household belongings, in search of greener pastures in the Garissa district of northern Kenya.*

the
LIFE AND SOUL

Kenya and Tanzania have a **remarkable diversity of people,** and it is they, just as much as the landscapes and wildlife, who represent the true spirit of the region. Whether rubbing shoulders with the hip city set, throwing dice with the unemployed in a shanty town or on a cultural visit in a rural setting, most visitors will tell you as much. Welcoming and affable, the local folk will readily share time and stories about life in East Africa, often following up with an invitation into their homes and villages.

By most estimates, Tanzania has close to 120 distinct ethnic groups and a number of less-defined ones, while Kenya has more than 70 different groups. Customs and beliefs play a role, but language is the primary distinguishing feature among them. Nevertheless language is nowadays also a binding factor, as Swahili has become the first language for almost 10 million people, particularly for those living along the coast. In the building of these nations, ethnic and cultural diversity have come about through a series of migrations from other parts of the continent as well as from outside of Africa. In Kenya, several major ethnic groups are well represented, comprising the Cushitic people, the Bantu-speakers and the Nilotic people. In Tanzania's case, over 95% of the population is of Bantu origin. The Swahili culture dominates the coast of both countries and the language, while classified as a Bantu one, draws from Arabic, Portuguese, Hindi and English.

During the 19th and 20th centuries, both countries saw the arrival of a variety of Asian and European immigrants, and although their populations remain relatively small, they have played an influential role in the history of both countries.

Previous spread: *A Maasai warrior (morani) will have his head shaved by his mother when he severs his ties with the warriorhood.*
Right: *The Hadzabe are regarded as Tanzania's earliest inhabitants.*
Opposite: *A Maasai child from the Loliondo District in Tanzania.*

Who's who in Tanzania?

No single group makes up more than 15% of the population, a fact that has ensured that throughout Tanzania's recent history, none has achieved political dominance and there has been almost no interethnic conflict. The following are some of the larger and better-known groups:

Sukuma – This Bantu-speaking group, comprising approximately 13% of the population, is the largest in Tanzania. Traditionally agriculturists, they are concentrated in the northern and western regions.

Nyamwezi – The second largest group, comprising just over 7% of the population, the Nyamwezi are closely related to the Sukuma and come from the same regions.

Chagga – Traditionally agriculturists, they settled the fertile lands on the southern slopes of Mt Kilimanjaro and down towards the Masai Steppe.

Haya – The Haya live around the edges of Lake Victoria. They are a Bantu-speaking group that comprises a number of sub-groups.

Makonde – This fiercely proud and independent Bantu-speaking group is thought to have moved up from Mozambique and settled in the southern regions of Tanzania and along the Ruvuma River. They are world-renowned as master carvers of wood.

Hadzabe and **Sandawe** – These two groups are regarded as Tanzania's earliest inhabitants. They both speak click languages and trace their heritage back over 10 000 years. The Hadzabe have settled around Lake Eyasi and the Sandawe in the central regions.

Maasai – With their red and blue robes and ornamental beadwork, these proud Nilotic cattle-herders are without doubt the most recognisable of all East Africa's people. In Tanzania, they are mostly found in the northern regions extending from the Serengeti down to the

northern edges of the Ruaha. The Tanzanian Maasai live a more traditional life than those in Kenya.

Iraqw – One of the smaller groups, the Iraqw have a Southern Cushitic heritage and are settled around Lake Eyasi and Lake Manyara.

Hadimu, Pemba and **Tumbatu** – These three groups comprise the majority of people living in the Zanzibar Archipelago. The Hadimu are from Zanzibar Island, while the Tumbatu and the Pemba hail from the islands of the same names.

Zinza – A small Bantu group who have settled in the area west of Lake Victoria, and on many of the islands in the lake itself.

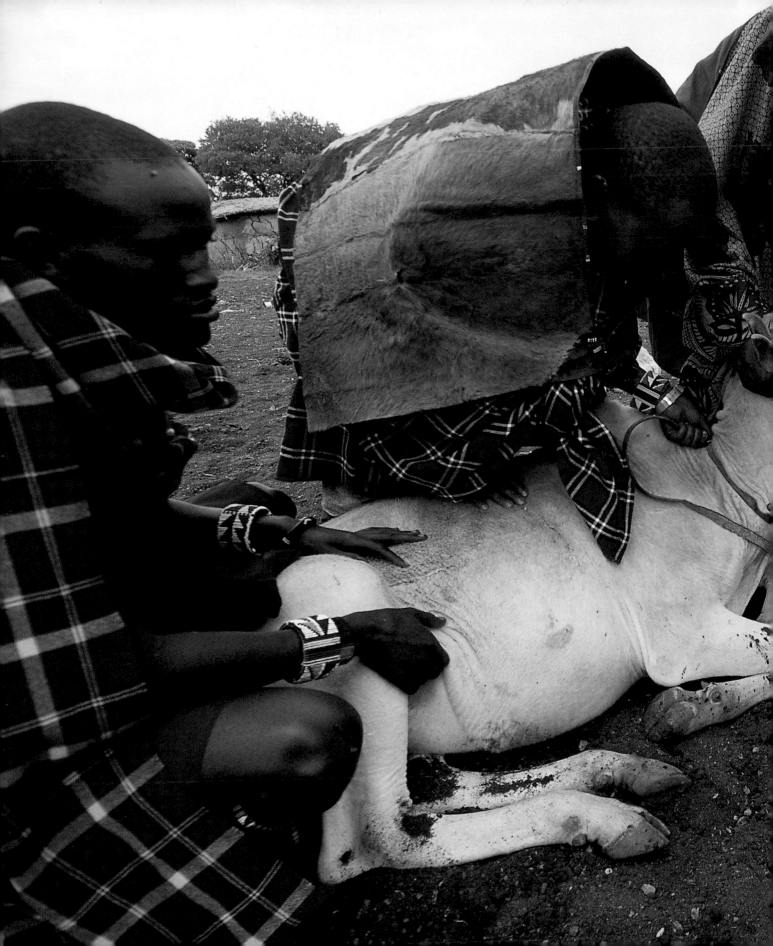

Left: *During a Maasai female circumcision ceremony, members of the initiate's family take blood from a cow for her to drink.*
Following spread: *Wangesha, a Samburu elder from the Kipsing district in northern Kenya.*
Page 174: *This Maasai warrior shows the typical braided hairstyle commonly worn by those within the age group.*
Page 175: *A typical flat-roofed Maasai hut is plastered with cow dung and mud. Family groups live together with a number of huts corralled in what are known locally as manyattas.*

Who's who in Kenya?

The Bantu and Nilotic people comprise the majority of Kenya's population with two groups, the Kikuyu and Luo, dominating in positions of power and influence. The country's European population retains more influence than their Tanzanian counterparts.

The following are some of the larger and better-known groups:

Kikuyu – This Bantu-speaking group is the largest, comprising almost 24% of the population. They have settled in the central regions between Nairobi and Mt Kenya. It was the Kikuyu who spearheaded the Mau Mau resistance movement against British colonial rule.

Luyha – The second-largest tribe is also Bantu-speaking and comprises a number of sub-groups that together make up almost 15% of the population. They traditionally come from the northern shores of Lake Victoria, stretching up along the border with Uganda.

Luo – The largest Nilotic-speaking clan, comprising 12% of the population. They came from Sudan and Chad and settled around the shores of Lake Victoria.

Kalenjin – Another Nilotic group that comprises a number of sub-groups, notably the Pokot, Kipsigis, Nandi and Tugen, who are spread through the Rift Valley regions north-west of Nairobi.

Kamba – These Bantu-speakers settled to the east of Nairobi towards Tsavo National Park. They arrived as hunters, but are now successful agriculturists.

Kisii – The Bantu-speaking Kisii have settled in the fertile south-western regions along the border with Tanzania.

Meru – The Meru are recognised as a Bantu tribe, but they have Cushitic and Nilotic influences. They have settled on the eastern slopes of Mt Kenya.

Bajun – Swahili-speaking Muslims from the Lamu Archipelago and the mainland coast opposite Lamu.

Mijikenda – Before the Arabs arrived, these Bantu-speaking people lived along the coastline from Malindi down to the border with Tanzania. They comprise at least eight smaller groups, but these tribes have splintered and their lineage has been diluted through intermarriage.

Maasai – As in Tanzania, the tribe best known to visitors. In Kenya, their traditional homeland extends from the Masai Mara up towards the central regions.

Samburu – Eastern Nilotic in origin, they are closely related to the Maasai. They speak the same language, and are probably the next most recognisable of East Africa's groups. Semi-nomadic pastoralists, they settled the drier lands north of Mt Kenya and up to Lake Turkana.

Turkana – These Eastern Nilotic people are found around the shores of Lake Turkana and towards the border with Uganda.

Orma – A Cushitic group of cattle- and camel-herders who live along the Tana River and in the drier regions around Garsen.

Rendille – Another camel-herding Cushitic group, neighbours to the Samburu in the dry north-east.

Left: *Maasai women from a craft co-operative on the outskirts of Tarangire.*
Opposite: *Swahili elders from the village of Watamau.*

So to speak

English and **Swahili** (Kiswahili) are the **official languages** of Tanzania and Kenya, and English is widely spoken in all cities and towns, popular hotels, lodges and stores, and in some form by those living in the rural areas. Minority languages include Hindi, Urdu and Arabic amongst the older generation in Zanzibar. Because of the number of Italian resort developments and visitors to the coastline, Italian has become something of a second language to those working in the tourist industry. It is not difficult to find Kenyan tour guides who are able to speak some Italian or German.

Swahili is classified as a Bantu language, and its purest forms are spoken in Zanzibar and along the Tanzanian coastline. The language has evolved through the centuries primarily as a common language for commerce, and the vocabulary has been influenced by the region's history of conquest and trade. Most linguists distinguish over **10 dialects** and some over 15. Kiunguja, the variant spoken in Zanzibar (which is also known as Unguja) and parts of mainland Tanzania, is accepted as the basis of **standard Swahili**. Before the arrival of Christian missionaries, the language was written in Arabic only; the first Swahili dictionary using the Roman alphabet appeared in the late 1800s. After Arabic, Swahili is the most widely-spoken language in Africa. Almost 10 million East Africans use it as their first language, and over 60 million as their second language.

Because of the large number of ethnic groups, there are over 150 indigenous languages spoken in East Africa. The major ones in Tanzania are those spoken by the Sukuma, Makonde and Chagga and in Kenya, by the Kikuyu, Maasai, Luo and Kikamba.

It is always agreeable to be able to greet the locals in their own language – so if you are venturing beyond the established tourist facilities and into the villages, on page 178 you'll find some words and phrases that should help to make your visit more pleasurable:

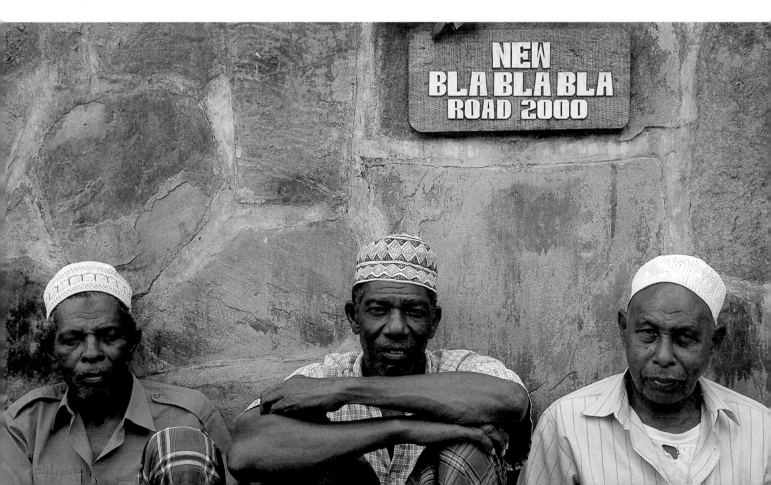

A traveller's vocabulary

General greeting – *Jambo*, or more informally, *Mambo*

When greeting elders with respect – *Shikamoo*

How are you? – *Hujambo?*, or more informally, *Habari?*

I am doing fine! – *Sijambo!* or more informally, *pao!*, which literally means 'cool'

Good or well – *Mzuri*

Fine – *Salama*

Good morning – *Habari za asubuhi*

Goodbye – *Kwaheri*

Good night – *Usiku mwema*

Thank you very much – *Asante sana*

Excuse me! – *Samahani!*

Please – *Tafadhali*

Yes – *Ndiyo*

No – *Hapana*

Is my vehicle really the 250th one to enter the Ngorongoro Crater today? – *Kweli gari yangu ndiyo ya mia mbili hamsini kuingia Ngorongoro Crater leo?*

I don't speak Swahili – *Sisemi Kiswahili*

Can you help me? – *Naomba msaada?*

What is your name? – *Jina lako ni nani?*

My name is Ali – *Jina lango ni Ali*

Why are Kenya's roads so shocking? – *Kwanini hali ya barabara za Kenya inatisha hivyo?*

What is the price? – *Bei gani?*

What time is it? – *Ni saa ngapi?*

Where is the toilet? – *Wapi choo?*

I don't care how cheap it is, I don't want to buy anything – *Sijali ni bei rahisi kiasi gani, sihitaji kununua chochote*

What is that animal? – *Huyo mnyama gani?*

Lion/giraffe/elephant/zebra/buffalo/leopard – *Simba/twiga/tembo/punda milia/nyati/ngwe*

Beach/mosque/church/market/bank – *Baharini/msikiti/kanisa/soko/benki*

Police station – *Kituo cha polisi*

Guesthouse/hotel – *Gesti/hoteli*

No, I am not going to offer you a bribe – *Hapana, sitakupa hongo*

Below: *Inside the home of an Orma family in northern Kenya.*

Myth and mystery of the Maasai

Of all East Africa's ethnic groups, none is better known than the Maasai. Fiercely proud and traditional people, these **semi-nomadic pastoralists** made their first forays into East Africa during the 15th century. They were known as fearsome warriors, and as they moved down the Nile River, coming south in search of grazing for their cattle, they forced many other tribes off the land along the way. Although they have been settled in the Great Rift Valley for centuries, the Maasai continue to expand their range beyond what is known as Maasailand.

Today, dressed in their characteristic conspicuous reds and blues, the Maasai are an integral part of the safari scene on the group ranches of Kenya and the tribal lands that surround the national parks of northern Tanzania. For the Maasai, their belief system, and life itself, is based on the ownership of cattle. These beasts are more than just a food source; they represent wealth and status. Even the legend that surrounds the origins of the five major clans is based on an initial distribution of red and black cattle. The present Maasai population is somewhere between 500 000 and 600 000, but their herds contain 3 to 4 million head of cattle. This is a number that is starting to cause concern, as many believe it is becoming unsustainable. But there is a positive side to this dedication to cattle; one that is rooted in the **mythology** of the Maasai people. They regard any wild animal as unequivocally inferior to domestic livestock, and particularly to cattle. So strong is this belief that the killing of any domestic animal by a wild beast is taken as a bad omen. A cow killed by a lion or elephant, for example, will not be eaten by the Maasai for fear of taking on the negative spirits within the dead animal. As long as you have cattle, as all traditional Maasai do, it is taboo to kill any wild animal or eat its meat. A Maasai tribesman who nevertheless does this is labelled an Ndorobo, a member of a despised local tribe. Because of these customs, wildlife has been spared wherever the Maasai have their traditional lands, notably in the Masai Mara and Serengeti and the surrounding areas.

There are many Maasai clans, and while all hold the same core beliefs regarding cattle and wild animals, the mythology surrounding these beliefs varies from clan to clan. The Laikipiak people from central Kenya have a particularly interesting belief as to how cattle came to be on Earth and how the Maasai became their keepers. The god Enkai is encountered in two forms: Enkai Narok, the giver of good, and Enkai Na-Nyokie, filled with anger and punishment. It was Enkai Narok who lowered the first **cattle from the heavens** upon a large cow hide. Enkai Narok also had three sons whom he set various tasks. The youngest son was given a hoe for digging and planting, and his offspring are the Kikuyu people of today. The second son was given a bow and arrow for hunting, and his offspring are the Kamba people. Finally, the first son was given a herding stick and told to mind the cattle, and his offspring are the Maasai. For the Laikipiak, owning cattle is a god-given right.

The Laikipiak also believe that certain wild animals owe their origins to domestic ones. They believe that buffalo have come from cattle that were given to women by Enkai but ran off into the wilds because they were neglected. In the same manner, gazelles are descended from goats, and warthogs from sheep.

Today, in some Maasai clans, anyone owning fewer than **50 head of cattle** is considered a poor man. A youngster will be sent out with his father's herd, and once he is able to look after cattle, usually by the age of 6 or 7, his parents will give him the first cows from which to build his own herd.

Certain wild animal species are given praise. All the clans see lion, for example, as a symbol of strength, so every warrior must spear a lion before becoming a junior elder. The Loita Clan in southern Kenya and northern Tanzania accords eland and impala a higher status than all other wild animals because they are regarded as early forms of cattle and goats.

The Maasai also hold the kudu in high esteem because of its horns, which are often used in their initiation ceremonies.

travel
DIRECTORY

Travel advisory

LOCAL TIME AND DIALLING CODES

Tanzania and Kenya use GMT (Greenwich Mean Time) plus 3 hours. There is no Daylight Saving Time. International dialling codes: Tanzania +255, Kenya +254 followed by area codes and telephone number. Outgoing dialling codes are 000 from both Tanzania and Kenya.

WHEN TO TRAVEL

East Africa offers good travelling conditions for most of the year, but the cooler and drier months from late June through early October are the most comfortable. The months of April and May, when the heavy rains fall, should be avoided, and November through to January can be uncomfortably hot along the coast and on the islands, especially if your accommodation has no air-conditioning. The peak tourism periods are the Christmas and New Year holiday break, and July through October when game viewing is at its best.

HEALTH AND MEDICINE

Tanzania and Kenya are classed as medium- to high-risk malaria countries; the risk of contracting the disease recedes with increasing altitude. Travellers must consult their local medical practitioners for advice on what malaria prophylaxis to take prior to departure. The only vaccination certificate that should be carried is for yellow fever. It is no longer necessary for entry into Tanzania and Kenya, but you may nevertheless be asked to produce it, and officials at your next destination will request it upon arrival. It is worth consulting your doctor about vaccinations for tetanus, polio, hepatitis A and B, typhoid, rabies and meningitis.

It is not advisable to drink any tap water in either country, or to eat uncooked foods that may have been washed in untreated water. Bottled water is readily available in all hotels, lodges and guesthouses as well as from most stores and restaurants. All cities have doctors and western medicines are available, but it is recommended that travellers take all basic medical requirements and specific medication with them. Most safari lodges and camps have comprehensive medical aid kits on their premises. It is advisable to carry adequate travel insurance, including cover for emergency air evacuation.

EMERGENCY SERVICE NUMBERS

Visitors should carry the contact details of their booking agents and ground operators with them at all times, as these numbers should be the first to be used in an emergency.

IN TANZANIA

IST Clinic (Dar es Salaam): +255 22 2601307 or 0744 783393 (mobile)
Aga Khan Hospital (Dar es Salaam): +255 22 2115151/3 or 0748 911111
AAR Medical Centre (Arusha): +255 27 2501593
Ambulance and Fire: 112

IN KENYA

Kenyan Tourist 24-hour Helpline: +254 20 604767
Nairobi Hospital: +254 20 2714400
Diani Beach Hospital: +254 40 2435

PUBLIC HOLIDAYS

1 January: New Year's Day – Kenya and Tanzania
12 January: Zanzibar Revolution Day – Tanzania only
March/April: Easter Weekend – Kenya and Tanzania
26 April: Union Day – Tanzania only
1 May: Labour Day – Kenya and Tanzania
1 June: Madaraka Day – Kenya only
7 July: Saba Saba (Traders' Day) – Tanzania only
8 August: Nane Nane (Farmers' Day) – Tanzania only
10 October: Moi Day – Kenya only
20 October: Kenyatta Day – Kenya only
9 December: Independence Day – Tanzania only
12 December: Independence Day – Kenya only
25 December: Christmas Day – Kenya and Tanzania
26 December: Boxing Day – Kenya and Tanzania

Islamic holidays are determined by phases of the moon and these will change from year to year. The important ones are Eid Al Hajj, Ramadan, Eid Al Fitr (the end of Ramadan) and Eid Al Maulid (Prophet Mohammed's birthday).

VISAS

Visitors from most countries require visas for Kenya and Tanzania; the exceptions are certain smaller Commonwealth countries. Visas are valid for up to three months per year and may be obtained at all major points of air or road entry. Fees are applicable for most countries. If you are planning to enter through one of the lesser-used border-posts, it is advisable to get your visa before travelling. Although obtaining a visa at the point of entry may be time-consuming, crossing the border is usually a formality, provided that you comply with all relevant laws. Currently, a visa issued in either Kenya and Tanzania is good for return visits between the two countries. A visa extension for either country can be obtained from the relevant immigration offices. These regulations do change, however, so it is always advisable to check with your agent before travelling.

SAFETY AND SECURITY

East Africa has over the last five years experienced some horrific and well-publicised incidents involving international terrorist groups, notably the US embassy bombings, which resulted in a dramatic decline in tourist numbers. Such events are unpredictable, and are more symptomatic of an unstable world order than of any instability in the region. East Africa remains generally a safe region in which to travel.

Tanzania annually records fewer incidents of crime than does Kenya. However, in the major urban areas of both countries, visitors should pay particular attention to the safety of their belongings and vehicles. Nairobi is particularly notorious for muggings and car-jackings, and some areas in Mombasa, Dar es Salaam and Arusha are prone to similar types of crime. Many of the coastal towns and the well-known beach destinations also experience petty theft. It is usually advisable to stick to recognised hotels, lodges and camp sites as these all have security measures in place. Visitors to Zanzibar should be aware of petty theft in Stone Town and along the beaches after dark.

Among the few irritations about travelling the region are the tourism touts who ply their illegal trade in all the major tourist cities, towns and beach destinations. Avoid them, no matter how enticing the safari, diving or excursion deal may sound, as the touts are often involved in criminal activities.

Because of banditry, travellers to northern Kenya should treat the far north-western parts towards the border with Sudan, and the north-eastern border with Somalia, as 'no go' areas. It is also advisable to do extensive research before crossing into Ethiopia by land.

KPMG (East Africa) runs a fraud and corruption hotline to assist the public and private sectors in an effort to curb corruption and economic crime. Visitors who are confronted with such incidents should contact zsheikh@kpmg.co.ke or mgaituri@kpmg.co.ke

CURRENCY AND BANKING

The international currencies of choice in the region are the US dollar, British pound and Euro. Cash is preferable, as travellers' cheques are exchanged at lower rates and a number of banks, tourist establishments and retail outlets will not accept them. The best places to exchange money are at exchange bureaux as they usually offer better rates. All major international credit cards are accepted in top-end establishments, but in many instances between 5 and 15% is added to the purchase price. Most local ATMs will accept VISA and Mastercard international credit cards. While all the major cities and most of the larger towns will have banking facilities, do not expect to find these in the smaller towns and rural areas.

Tanzania's unit of currency is the Tanzanian shilling, while that of Kenya is the Kenyan shilling. There are no restrictions on currency movements conducted by visitors.

ELECTRICITY

All regions in East Africa are supplied with 220-240 volts AC, although lodges in outlying areas will usually have independent power generators. Most plugs and sockets are of the British three-square-pin 13-amp format. Adaptors are available for purchase in city and town stores and for guest use in all hotels and lodges.

FEES FOR PARKS AND RESERVES

Fees are charged for visiting national parks and reserves. Both Tanzania and Kenya have a US dollar-based fee structure for non-residents and a cheaper local currency rate for residents and citizens. The rates per 24-hour period are higher for the larger, more popular parks, and there is an additional per-day charge for those travelling by private vehicle. These fees change annually, so it is best to consult the respective national bodies for the latest charges.

In Kenya, access to the major parks is by way of a Smartcard issued at KWS head office in Nairobi, or at the main gates only of certain parks. If you are travelling by road, it is advisable to pre-purchase these cards or access may be denied. If you are travelling on a pre-booked package, entry fees are included.

TRAVEL TIPS
• In both Tanzania and Kenya, the unfortunate reality is that dealing with official bodies such as the tourism boards and national airlines can be extremely frustrating. Phones are not answered, information is not available and there is often little genuine effort to help. The answer is to make use of private sector companies and operators, as they are far more efficient and will usually make the effort to get you all the relevant information when you are planning a trip.
• For those travelling by road, a *carnet de passage* for the vehicle is a necessity, as it will exempt you from paying import duties. It is also best to travel with an international driving license. Vehicle insurance will have to be purchased at entry points. Carry these documents at all times.
• All the major cities, safari towns and beach destinations in both Tanzania and Kenya are full of touts and back-street operators. Do not get taken in by offers of cheap trips and make sure you conduct all bookings with a recognized and licensed operator. Avoid changing money with street touts.
• Cell phones are extremely popular throughout East Africa, and starter packs and prepaid vouchers are available in every urban area. If you are spending an extended period in the country, consider buying a local number. It is possible to hire cell phones in all major cities and resorts.
• Do not take photographs of sensitive government buildings such as residences, military barracks and airports or of any officials in uniform.

• In Zanzibar, Pemba, Lamu and most of the coastal cities and towns of both countries, the Islamic faith is the dominant religion. Followers adhere to fairly well-defined expectations of social conduct and it is common courtesy to respect their customs regarding dress codes and alcohol consumption. While most people are extremely friendly, ask permission before taking photographs, especially of women, and don't enter mosques without permission and before having taken your shoes off.
• The airports in both countries can be a little confusing. In Kenya, the main international airport is Jomo Kenyatta International, but almost all safaris will be scheduled in and out of Wilson Airport. In Tanzania, the safari industry is mostly based in Arusha, and there are two airports roughly equidistant from the town. Most international flights will fly into Kilimanjaro International Airport, and most safaris are scheduled out of Arusha Airport, but sometimes these roles may be switched. Always double-check which airports you are due to fly in and out of.
• If you are travelling by road, a reliable place for servicing is Ndovu Holdings in the industrial area of Nairobi – contact Martzio Kravos on +254 722 515132.

WANT TO READ MORE?
The Circle of Life by Anup and Manoj Shah
Kilimanjaro – To the Roof of Africa by Audrey Salkeld
Maasai by Tepilit Ole Saitoti and Carol Beckwith
The Oral Literature of The Maasai by Naomi Kipury
Samburu by Nigel Pavitt
Tanzania – Portrait of a Nation by Paul Joynson-Hicks
Africa's Great Rift Valley by Nigel Pavitt
Wildlife Wars by Dr Richard Leakey
Africa: A Biography of the Continent by John Reader
Kenya – Lonely Planet Guide
Tanzania – Lonely Planet Guide
Journey through Kenya by Mohammed Amin, Duncan Willets and Brian Tetley
Journey through Tanzania by Mohammed Amin, Duncan Willets and Brian Tetley
Zanzibar – The Insider's Guide by Ian Michler
The Great Migration by Carlo Mari and Harvey Croze

Contact details – Tanzania

TOURISM REPRESENTATIVES

Tanzania Tourism Board (Dar es Salaam): PO Box 2485, Dar es Salaam. Tel: +255 22 2111244/5, e-mail: md@ttb.ud.or.tz or safari@ud.co.tz, website: www.tanzania-web.com

Tanzania Tourism Board (Arusha): PO Box 2348, Arusha. Tel: +255 27 2503842/3, e-mail: ttb-info@habari.co.tz

Tanzania National Parks (TANAPA): PO Box 3134, Arusha. Tel: +255 27 2504082, e-mail: tanapa@habari.co.tz

Air Tanzania: PO Box 543, Dar es Salaam. Tel: +255 22 2110245/8 or 2118411, e-mail: tanzanair@raha.com, website: www.airtanzania.com

Zanzibar Commission for Tourism: PO Box 1410, Zanzibar Town. Tel: +255 747 2233485, e-mail: zanzibartourism@zanzibartourism.net, website: zanzibartourism.net

TOUR AND SAFARI OPERATORS

Invent Africa: Unit A1, Westlake Square, Westlake Drive, Tokai, 7945 Cape Town, South Africa. Tel: +27 21 7011179, e-mail: reservations@inventafrica.com, website: www.inventafrica.com

Nomad Tanzania: PO Box 681, Usa River, Arusha. Tel: +255 27 2553819/20, e-mail info@nomad.co.tz, website: www.nomad-tanzania.com

The Selous Safari Company: PO Box 1192, Dar es Salaam. Tel: +255 22 2134794, e-mail: info@selous.com, website: www.selous.com

Sanctuary Lodges: PO Box 427, Arusha. Tel: +255 27 2509816/7, e-mail: tanzania@sanctuarylodges.com, website: www.sanctuarylodges.com

Asilia Lodges & Camps: PO Box 2657, Arusha. Tel: +255 748 888975, e-mail: info@asilia.com, website: www.asilialodges.com

CC Africa: Private Bag X27, Benmore, 2010, Johannesburg, South Africa. Tel: +27 11 8094300, e-mail: information@ccafrica.com, website: www.ccafrica.com

African Safari Roots: 3 Bowjey Terrace, Newlyn, Cornwall, UK, TR185NY. Tel: +44 1736 367635, e-mail: rob@africansafariroots.com, website: www.africansafariroots.com

Foxes of Africa: PO Box 10270, Dar es Salaam. Tel: +255 744 237422, e-mail: fox@tanzaniasafaricamps.info, website: www.tanzaniasafaris.com

Protea Hotels: International Central Reservations. Tel: +27 21 4305000, e-mail: sto@proteahotels.com, website: www.proteahotels.com

HOTELS AND LODGES

Chada Katavi (see Nomad Tanzania)

Greystoke Mahale (see Nomad Tanzania)

Sand Rivers Selous (see Nomad)

Selous Safari Camp (see Selous Safari Company)

Ras Kutani (see Selous Safari Company)

Jongomeru Camp (see Selous Safari Company)

Swala Camp (see Sanctuary Lodges)

Lake Manyara Tree Lodge (see CC Africa)

Ngorongoro Crater Lodge (see CC Africa)

Kleins Camp (see CC Africa)

Grumeti River (see CC Africa)

Sayari Camp (see Asilia Lodges)

Mullers Mountain Lodge: PO Box 34, Lushoto. Tel: +255 27 2640204, e-mail: mullersmountainlodge@yahoo.com

Kisima Ngeda: PO Box 2590, Arusha. Tel: +255 27 2534128, e-mail: kisima@habari.co.tz

Mwagusi Safari Camp: PO Box 369, Iringa, e-mail: chrisfox@bushlink.co.tz, website: www.ruaha.org

Saadani Safari Lodge: PO Box 105854, Dar es Salaam. Tel: +255 22 2773294, e-mail: info@saadani.net, website: www.saadani.net

The Tides: PO Box 46, Pangani. Tel: +255 741 325812, e-mail: thetides@thetideslodge.com, website: www.thetideslodge.com

Protea Amaani Beach (see Protea Hotels)

Highland Lodge (see Foxes of Africa)

Lazy Lagoon (see Foxes of Africa)

MOBILE OPERATORS
Nomad Tanzania: PO Box 681, Usa River, Arusha. Tel: +255 27 2553819/20, e-mail: info@nomad.co.tz, website: www.nomad-tanzania.com
Wild Frontiers: PO Box 844, Halfway House, 1685 South Africa. Tel: +27 11 7022035, e-mail: wildfront@icon.co.za, website: www.wildfrontiers.com

AIR CHARTER
Regional Air: PO Box 14755, Arusha. Tel: +255 27 2504477 or 744 285753, e-mail: sales@regional.co.tz, website: www.airkenya.com

INVESTMENT OPPORTUNITIES
National Development Corporation: PO Box 2669, Dar es Salaam. Tel: +255 22 2112893, e-mail: ndc@cats-net.com
Confederation of Tanzania Industries (CTI): PO Box 71783, Dar es Salaam. Tel: +255 2114954, e-mail: cti@cti.co.tz, website: www.ctitz.com
The Tanzania Investment Centre (TIC): website: www.tic.co.tz

Contact details - Kenya

TOURISM REPRESENTATIVES
Kenyan Tourist Board (Nairobi): PO Box 30630, Nairobi. Tel: +254 20 719924/26/28, e-mail: info@kenyatourism.org, website: www.kenyatourism.org
Kenyan Tourist Board (Mombasa): Moi International Airport. Tel: +254 41 433211/433229
Kenya Association of Tour Operators: PO Box 48461, Nairobi. Tel: +254 20 713386/713348, e-mail: info@katokenya.org, website: www.katokenya.org
Kenya Tourism Federation: PO Box 15013, Nairobi. Tel: +254 20 604729/30
Kenya Airways: PO Box 4101, Nairobi. Tel: +254 20 32074100, website: www.kenya-airways.com

TOUR AND SAFARI OPERATORS
Invent Africa: Unit A1, Westlake Square, Westlake Drive, Tokai, 7945 Cape Town, South Africa. Tel: +27 21 7011179, e-mail: reservations@inventafrica.com, website: www.inventafrica.com
Robert & William Carr-Hartley Safaris: PO Box 24773, Nairobi. Tel: +254 20 890335 or 722 510673, e-mail: robert@carrhartley.com, website: www.carrhartley.com

Private Wilderness: PO Box 6648, GPO 00100, Nairobi, Kenya. Tel: +254 20 882028/882598, e-mail: info@privatewilderness.com, website: www.privatewilderness.com
Cheli & Peacock: PO Box 743-00517, Nairobi. Tel: +254 20 603090, e-mail: safaris@chelipeacock.co.ke, website: www.chelipeacock.co.ke
CC Africa: Private Bag X27, Benmore, 2010 Johannesburg, South Africa. Tel: +27 11 8094300, e-mail: information@ccafrica.com, website: www.ccafrica.com
African Safari Roots: 3 Bowjey Terrace, Newlyn, Cornwall, UK, TR185NY. Tel: +44 1736 367635, e-mail: rob@africansafariroots.com, website: www.africansafariroots.com

MOBILE OPERATORS
Robert & William Carr-Hartley Safaris: PO Box 24773, Nairobi. Tel: +254 20 890335 or 722 510673, e-mail: robert@carrhartley.com, website: www.carrhartley.com
Bill Winter Safaris: PO Box 24871, Nairobi. Tel: +254 20 883369, e-mail: bill.winter@africaonline.co.ke, website: www.bwsafaris.com

LODGES AND HOTELS

Bateleur Camp (see CC Africa)
Elsa's Kopje (see Cheli & Peacock)
Naro Moru River Lodge: PO Box 18, Naro Moru. Tel: +254 62 62023/62212, e-mail: alliance@africaonline.co.ke
Ol Donyo Wuas: PO Box 56923, Nairobi. Tel: 254 20 600457, e-mail: info@bush-and-beyond.com, website: www.richardbonhamsafaris.com
Kilalinda (see Private Wilderness)
Rusinga Island Lodge (see Private Wilderness)
Bedouin Camp (see Private Wilderness)
Hippo Point: PO Box 1852, Naivasha. Tel: +254 50 2021295, e-mail: hippo-pt@africaonline.co.ke, website: www.hippo-pointkenya.com
Pinewood Village: E-mail: pinewood@africaonline. co.ke, website: www.pinewood-village.com
Diani House: PO Box 5002-80401, Diani Beach. Tel: +254 40 32034872, e-mail: aceltd@africaonline.co.ke or info@dianihouse.com, website: www.dianihouse.com
Man Friday: PO Box 592, Malindi. Tel: +254 721 734171, e-mail: skanderson30@hotmail.com
Himaya House: Malindi. Tel: +254 42 30745, e-mail: lissa@africaonline.co.ke
Manada Bay: PO Box 144, Lamu. Tel: +254 42 633475 or 722 203108/9, e-mail: bookings@mandabay.com, website: www.mandabay.com
Salama and Azania House: PO Box 471, Lamu. Tel: +254 42 633491, e-mail: info@lamuworld. com, website: www.lamuworld.com
Loisaba (see Cheli & Peacock)
Borana: PO Box 477, Nanyuki. Tel: +254 20 600457 or 722 207717, e-mail: info@bush-and-beyond.com, website: www.borana.com
Lewa Downs: PO Box 10607-00100, Nairobi. Tel: +254 20 600457, e-mail: info@bush-and-beyond.com, website: www.lewa.org

Shompole: PO Box 10665-00100, Nairobi. Tel: +254 20 884135/883280, e-mail: info@shompole.com, website: www.shompole.com
Finch Hattons: PO Box 24423, Nairobi. Tel: +254 20 310335/6, e-mail: finchhattons@iconnect.co.ke, website: www.finchhattons.com
Tortilis Camp (see Cheli & Peacock)
Tamarind Village: Tel: +254 41 474600/1, e-mail: info@tamarindmsa.co.ke, website: www.tamarind.co.ke
The Cove: PO Box 5016, Diani. E-mail: cro@africa-renaissance.com, website: www.cove.co.ke

WALKING SAFARIS

Insiders Africa: PO Box 24133, Nairobi. Tel: +254 721 242361, e-mail: alex.hunter@swiftkenya.com, website: www.insidersafrica.com
Phil West Safaris: PO Box 18559-00500, Nairobi, Kenya. Tel: +254 20 891063, e-mail: phil@bilwestsafaris.com

DIVING OPERATORS

Pilli Pipa Dhow Safari: PO Box 5185, Diani Beach. Tel: +254 40 3202401/3203559, e-mail: info@pillipipa.com, website: www.pillipipa.com
Aqua Ventures: PO Box 275, Watamu. Tel: +254 42 32420, e-mail: aquav@africaonline.co.ke, website: www.duveinkenya.com

AIR CHARTER

Air Kenya: PO Box 30357, 00100, Nairobi. Tel: +254 20 605745, e-mail: resvns@airkenya.com, website: www.airkenya.com

INVESTMENT OPPORTUNITIES

Kenya Association of Manufacturers: PO Box 30225-00100 GPO, Nairobi. Tel: +254 20 3746005, e-mail: info@kam.co.ke, website: www.kam.co.ke

Index

Page numbers in *italics* refer to photographs.

To travel with Ian as your guide or receive advice on travel in Southern or East Africa, you can contact him at:

INVENT AFRICA
Tel: +27 21 7011179
e-mail: reservations@inventafrica.com
website: www.inventafrica.com

Ian Michler, a stockbroker by profession, left the world of finance in 1989 to live and work with the spunky cartographer Tessa van Schaik in the Okavango. He has 15 years of guiding experience, mostly in Botswana, Namibia, Zimbabwe and East Africa – conducting big game, birding, adventure and photographic safaris. When not on safari, he works as a photojournalist, writing on conservation, wildlife, and travel issues, mainly for Africa Geographic and Africa – Birds & Birding. He has worked as a researcher and field co-ordinator on numerous natural history television documentaries. Ian has four previous books to his credit: *This is Mozambique, Mozambique – A Visual Souvenir, Botswana – The Insider's Guide* and *Zanzibar – The Insider's Guide*. He is a past category winner in the Agfa Wildlife Photographic Awards. He is presently based in Cape Town, South Africa, where he is a partner in a safari company offering specialist guided trips.

I have been able to complete this project thanks to the invaluable assistance and support of others. Many of these people are doing exemplary work, and play important roles in the success of the region. My thanks and heartfelt gratitude go especially to Eliza Deacon in Arusha, Mark and Claire Jenkins in Meru National Park, Angela Sheldrick and Rob Carr-Hartley in Nairobi National Park, and Suzie Reading in Nairobi for opening their homes and personal contact books to me, and for playing such enthusiastic and supportive roles.

In Tanzania, I want to thank: Mark Holdsworth, Roland Purcell, Richard and Jules Knocker and Uli and Stephanie Kuerzinger from Nomad Tanzania, Chris and Nani Schmelling from Kisima Ngeda, Charles Dobie and Hein and Alison Prinsloo from Selous Safari Company, Chris Fox from Mwagusi Safari Camp, Robert Glen and Susan Stolberger in Ruaha National Park, Dr Peter Morkel from the Frankfurt Zoological Society, Jason King from CC Africa, Julian Camm from Sanctuary Lodges, Coenraad Bantjes from Saadani Safari Lodge, Gino Sieni from Protea Hotels, and Caroline Blumer from Regional Air. And to Lizzie Farren, Hugo Titley, James Powell and Annabelle Ross for the party times in and around Arusha.

In Kenya, my gratitude goes to: Ava Paton and Andrea Maggie from Elsa's Kopje, Andy and Caragh Roberts from Manda Bay, Ed Jarvis from Hippo Point, Nicky Parazzi from Watamu, Stefano Chelie from Chelie Peacock, Karin Bernadi from Private Wilderness, Martzio Kravos from Ndovu Holdings, JB Ong'uti of Alliance Hotels, Nicky Young, Patrick Stanton and Richard and Tara Bonham from Ol Donyo Wuas, Lissa Ruben from Malindi, Craig and Samantha Griffiths from Bedouin Camp, Fuzz and Bimbi Dyer from Borana Lodge, Ian Craig from Lewa Downs, Tom Sylvester from Loisaba, Joseph Masibo at Bateleur Camp, Anthony Russell from Shompole, Justin Tilley from Pinewood Village and Hans Strijdom from Ali Barbour's Cave.

Also to Shayne Richardson at CC Africa, Rob McDowell at African Safari Roots for his pre-trip advice, Charles Spencer for being a superb shopping partner and for provoking my near arrest at Mombasa Airport, and Ian and Sharon McCallum and Ian McMillan and Robbyn Moir from Invent Africa. There were also a great many people I met along the way who shared their stories and wisdom; you have all helped in some way to shape this book.

At Struik Publishers, to Dominique le Roux and Lesley Hay-Whitton, editor Helen de Villiers, Hirt & Carter's Danny Michelini and the rest of the production team: thanks for your creativity and hard work. Thanks to Tessa for her wonderful artwork.

First published in 2006 by Struik Publishers
(a division of New Holland Publishing (South Africa) (Pty) Ltd)
New Holland Publishing is a member of Johnnic Communications Ltd

Garfield House, 86–88 Edgware Road, London W2 2EA, United Kingdom
www.newhollandpublishers.com

80 McKenzie Street, Cape Town 8001, South Africa www.struik.co.za

14 Aquatic Drive, Frenchs Forest, NSW 2086, Australia

218 Lake Road, Northcote, Auckland, New Zealand

ISBN 1 77007 011 7 (9 781770 070110)

1 3 5 7 9 10 8 6 4 2

Publishing manager: Dominique le Roux
Managing editor: Lesley Hay-Whitton
Editor: Helen de Villiers
Designer: Daniele Michelini
Concept designer: Alison Day
Cartographer: Tessa van Schaik
Proofreader: Irma van Wyk
Indexer: Ethné Clarke

Reproduction by Hirt & Carter Cape (Pty) Ltd
Printed and bound by Kyodo Printing Co (S'pore) Pte Ltd, Singapore